W9-AGE-954

GLORIOUS LIQUEURS

NEW COUNTRY FARE

GLORIOUS LIQUEURS

150 RECIPES FOR SPIRITED DESSERTS, DRINKS, AND GIFTS OF FOOD

Edited by MARY AUREA MORRIS
Recipes by CERI HADDA
Photography by ELIZABETH WATT

LAKE
ISLE
PRESS, INC.

NEW YORK

Published by Lake Isle Press, Inc.
2095 Broadway, New York, NY 10023
Distributed by Publishers Group West
Emeryville, CA

Photographs copyright © 1988, 1990, and 1991
by Elizabeth Watt
Recipes copyright © 1991 by Ceri Hadda with the exception of the following: Vanilla Cordial is reprinted with the permission of the American Spice Trade Association; the recipes for Orange Liqueur, Coffee Liqueur, Almond Liqueur, and Raspberry Brandy appear by kind permission of Daphne Metaxas Hartwig.

Certain of these recipes were previously published in *Victoria*, *Food & Wine* and *Food and Wines of France*.

LIBRARY OF CONGRESS CATALOG CARD NUMBER: 91-60332

ISBN-0-9627403-1-4

Book Design: Mary Moriarty

September 1991

10 9 8 7 6 5 4 3 2 1

In memory of George Hadda,
who loved liqueurs

CONTENTS

INTRODUCTION

From the time I was a little girl, I wholeheartedly espoused the oft-heard adage that first impressions count. And, as I grew up and learned to cook, I soon discovered the motto was as true of preparing food as it was of anything else—one flat soufflé could forever ruin one's reputation as a competent chef. Yet happily for me, my mother was an enterprising aficionado of fine food who introduced me to the world of liqueurs and the magic they worked with a menu. Before long I realized that whenever I served liqueur-laced desserts, it didn't matter what course had come first—or how it had turned out—my splendid finale always made the impression that counted.

Liqueurs have long had a royal reputation, and once you have made them part of your own repertoire, you'll understand why. They make a princely addition to many dishes, transforming an ordinary meal into an extraordinary feast. But because they are sweet, their special charms are best reserved for treats—delicious drinks, marvelous mousses, and cakes and pies befitting a banquet. Christen any confection with a liqueur and it becomes excitingly eloquent, be it ordinary ice cream, a simple beverage, a modest jar of jam. Whether a liqueur is the only added ingredient or one of many, it imparts a pleasingly rich flavor to the foods it's paired with. Think of liqueurs as lively and animated, the adventurous members of a very spirited family.

Despite their exotic names and equally exotic histories, liqueurs (or cordials as they are also known) are easy to define: They are sweetened spirits (whiskey, vodka, brandy, and rum are all used) infused with fruit, herbs, nuts, or spices. Although such classic varieties as Amaretto and Grand Marnier are among the finest in the world, their production lovingly nurtured and closely guarded, it is not difficult to make your own, and, in fact, in Glorious Liqueurs we tell you how. Admittedly the homemade versions are not exact equivalents of the more venerable potions, but they do boast some definite advantages. For one thing, they are less expensive; for another, their taste may be adjusted to your own—stronger or weaker, sweeter or drier. Creating liqueurs is fun, too, a pleasurable prelude to the dessert- and drink-making to come.

Steeping herbs and plants in alcohol dates from antiquity, when Hippocrates among others recognized their digestive and healing properties. However, liqueurs as we know them today were developed much later, during the Middle Ages in European monasteries. Christian monks, often secluded yet sought out by the populace for medical advice, began experimenting with existing alchemy formulas, producing remedies for all sorts of ills. These early mixtures were bitter, to be sure, but the introduction of sweeter herbs and syrups vastly improved palatability, and eventually pursuing good health became a sensual pastime. Today's elixirs are drunk primarily for pleasure, yet to many they are still a serendipitous aide to well-being.

In Glorious Liqueurs we take you on a journey to the enticing land of liqueur-filled confections: delectable hot and cold drinks, tempting cakes and pies, irresistible cookies and candies. If compotes and crepes are to your liking, we have those, too, plus puddings, some mousses, even an elegant soufflé. There is also a chapter on ice cream, an all-American favorite decked out in fancy new dress. And for gifts that speak sweet thoughts, turn to the section on presents from the pantry—these condiments and conserves are worthy of any friend.

Throughout these pages food expert Ceri Hadda has included sweets for every inclination. Whether you favor fruit and spices, as I do, or coffee and chocolate, as Ceri does, you'll discover a tantalizing selection of recipes. Perhaps you'll like the Chambord Linzer Torte (one of my favorites), a heavenly swirl of raspberry preserves in a luscious nutty dough, or the Banana Coffee Cake, a feathery cake crowned with nuts and coconut. The Black Currant Tea and Cassis Brownies might appeal to you as much as they do Ceri; fruit and chocolate meet in one of the happiest food marriages imaginable. When your appetite demands that you indulge, you will find it hard to pick your poison. Ceri sometimes turns to the sinfully rich Cranberry Sacher Torte; you might too.

As you browse through this book, note that there are recipes for every timetable. Many are very easy to execute, involving only one or two steps, while others are more detailed, with liqueur the star ingredient of a large cast. Either way, they are eminently adaptable, often succeeding as well with one liqueur as they do with another. Try the alternatives we suggest or experiment yourself— chances are, your version will be just as delicious.

After you have sampled a dessert or two, I hope you will share my obvious enthusiasm. Liqueurs are, after all, sweet and happy spirits synonymous with good food and good times. And when you think of it, what could possibly please a hostess more?

Mary Aurea Morris

LIST OF LIQUEURS

This list is neither comprehensive nor generic. It contains liqueurs used in the recipes in this book. Some of the liqueurs cited below are generic names; others are proprietary.

Alizé: An opaque orange liqueur with the pronounced, fresh flavor of passion fruit blended with Cognac. It adds a brilliant note to orange juice.

Anisette: Flavored with licorice-like anise, a clear or red liqueur that's often splashed into a cup of espresso coffee.

Amaretto di Saronno: Deriving its bitter almond flavor from apricot pits (like amaretti cookies), a honey-colored liqueur.

B & B: Proprietary name for a blend of Bénédictine and brandy. Owing to the brandy, this is less sweet than many liqueurs.

Bénédictine: Infused with herbs, plants, and peels, this amber liqueur was created by Bénédictine monks in the sixteenth century. Its mildly medicinal flavor is not to everyone's liking.

Chambord: A luscious, fragrant raspberry and honey liqueur that is quintessential berry!

Chartreuse: Available in green (110 proof), yellow (80 proof), and ALC (108 proof and rarely available) varieties, this liqueur is reportedly fortified with a mysterious blend of 130 alpine herbs. Like Bénédictine, it is created by monks, this time Carthusian monks from La Grande Chartreuse near Grenoble, France. This is the only liqueur to have a color named after it, but that still does not make it the most appealing flavor to all palates.

Cherry Heering: This is the proprietary name for a Danish cherry liqueur. It is faintly reminiscent of cherry coffee syrup, but surprisingly appealing nonetheless.

Cherry Suisse: From the manufacturers of Vandermint comes this liqueur with the flavors of a chocolate-covered cherry. Delicious over cherry ice cream, garnished with chocolate curls.

Cointreau: This classic French liqueur blends sweet and bitter Mediterranean and tropical orange peels. It tastes slightly less sweet than Grand Marnier.

Crème de cacao: Available in white and brown varieties, which have the same taste, this is an appealing liqueur that blends the flavor of cocoa beans with a touch of vanilla. The white variety is used with green crème de menthe, to create Grasshoppers.

Crème de cassis: This garnet-colored liqueur is made from black currants, primarily around the Dijon region of France. It is unusual among liqueurs in that it's used as an apéritif, Kir, which combines white wine with a splash of cassis.

Crème de menthe: The white and green varieties of this mouthwash-like liqueur have the same flavor. Distilled from several varieties of mint, notably peppermint, this liqueur is particularly refreshing when poured over a glass of crushed ice.

Curaçao: From the Dutch West Indies comes this orange-flavored liqueur that is sometimes colored swimming pool blue. Lower in proof than Triple Sec, it's flavored with dried peel from local green oranges.

Drambuie: Proprietary brand name for a Scotch whisky-based liqueur flavored with heather honey and spices. The national liqueur of Scotland.

Eggnog: A thick, creamy egg-based liqueur, often made in Holland.

Fraise des bois: Flavored with wild strawberries, an intensely true-to-the-fruit liqueur.

Framboise: Raspberry-flavored liqueur, similar to cassis.

Frangelico: So purely flavored, you'll think you're drinking liquid hazelnuts! Named for the hermit who supposedly crafted the recipe using wild hazelnuts.

Fruit liqueurs: Flavored and colored with the fruit of choice, these are lower proof and sweeter than comparable fruit-flavored brandies.

Fruit brandies: Like fruit liqueurs, flavored and colored with the fruit of choice. In this case, however, always 70 proof.

Grand Marnier: Proprietary name for a classic French orange liqueur based on Cognac. Deeply flavored with the peels of wild bitter oranges, this liqueur's fragrance is tantamount to perfume.

Irish Cream Liqueur: Fresh Irish cream, whiskey, and hints of coconut and caramel round out this creamy liqueur, delicious as an ingredient, substantial enough to make an instant topping. Serve chilled, on the rocks, or at room temperature.

Irish Mist: Similar to Drambuie, this liqueur is based on whiskey and sweetened with honey.

Kahlúa: From Mexico comes this espresso-colored, coffee-flavored liqueur, which does much to enhance coffee and other drinks, as well as desserts.

La Grande Passion: From the manufacturers of Grand Marnier, a passion fruit liqueur based on Armagnac. Not as sweet tasting as Alizé, it is appropriate for use in both before- and after-dinner drinks.

Liqueur Brûlé: A caramel liqueur with a buttery nuance.

Liquore Galliano: Golden Italian liqueur in a long-necked bottle. Distilled from seeds, herbs, and spices, it's often poured into orange juice to make Harvey Wallbanger cocktails.

Liquore Strega: An Italian liqueur with a lively citrus quality and golden color.

Lochan Ora: From Scotland, this Scotch-based liqueur is quietly flavored with ingredients from the West Indies and Sri Lanka.

Mandarine Napoleon: Tangerines and Cognac flavor this amber liqueur.

Midori: Bright green like the honeydew it's flavored with, this Japanese liqueur is refreshingly true to the fruit. (Midori means "green" in Japanese.)

Nocello: Rich with walnut flavor, useful in any recipe calling for the nut's rich character.

Opal Nera: An ebony-colored 80-proof Italian sambuca. Flavored with anise and elderflower with a wisp of lemon.

Ouzo: This clear Greek liqueur is anise-flavored, but it's not as sweet, and it's stronger than regular anisette. Like Pernod, it turns opalescent when mixed with water.

Pernod: The color of an unripe lime, this anise-flavored liqueur turns milky white when mixed with water and ice.

Sabra: From Israel, this chocolate-flavored liqueur is intriguingly accented with Jaffa oranges.

Sambuca Romana: Deriving its licorice flavor from elder bush fruit, this liqueur is classically added to espresso along with three coffee beans.

Sloe Gin: Highlighted in the sloe gin fizz, this red liqueur is flavored with cherry-like sloeberries.

Southern Comfort: This potent peach-flavored liqueur has a bourbon whiskey base.

Tiá Maria: Coffee liqueur from Jamaica with a rum-flavored base.

Triple Sec: Another orange-flavored liqueur, this one, flavored with orange peel from the Dutch West Indies, is reminiscent of curaçao but it's clear, plus sweeter and higher in proof than curaçao.

Truffles: Like its confectionery namesake, this chocolate liqueur has nutty nuances.

Tuaca: Italy's orange liqueur, with a whiff of vanilla.

Vandermint: Sold in a Delft-like bottle, this Dutch liqueur combines chocolate and mint to make a refreshing treat.

RECIPES FOR ALL SEASONS

Cranberry Cordial • Orange Liqueur

Raspberry Liqueur • Almond Liqueur

Hazelnut Liqueur • Crème De Menthe

Vanilla Cordial • Chocolate Liqueur

Coffee Liqueur • Cinnamon Spice Liqueur

Piña Colada Cream Liqueur

Mocha Cream Liqueur

CRANBERRY CORDIAL

A brilliantly colored cordial that's nice for sipping after the holiday meal, neat or over crushed ice. It's also a treat over ice cream.

MAKES ABOUT 3 PINTS

8 cups raw cranberries, coarsely chopped
6 cups sugar
1 bottle (1 liter) light or amber rum

Place the chopped cranberries in a gallon jar with a tight-fitting cover (or divide between two half-gallon jars). Add the sugar and the rum. Close the jar tightly; shake gently to blend. Store in a cool, dark place for 6 weeks, stirring or shaking the contents every day. Strain the cordial into decorative bottles. Seal with corks.

NOTE: The recipe can be halved or even quartered. For a half recipe, use 4 cups cranberries, 3 cups sugar, and 2 1/2 cups rum; for a quarter recipe, use 2 cups cranberries, 1 1/2 cups sugar, and 1 1/4 cups rum.

8 cran
8 sugar 5 c vodka

ORANGE LIQUEUR

A liqueur you can make all year round.

MAKES ABOUT 1 1/2 PINTS

4 medium navel oranges

1 medium lemon

3 cups vodka

1 1/2 cups superfine sugar, purchased or homemade (see Note)

8 drops yellow food coloring (optional)

1 drop red food coloring (optional)

1 teaspoon glycerine (optional thickener)

Rinse and dry the oranges and the lemon. Use the shredding side of a cheese grater to scrape only the orange part off the oranges; be careful not to scrape off the white, bitter part. Scrape the peel off half the lemon in the same way. Put the orange and lemon zests in a glass jar; add the vodka. Seal tightly and let steep for 3 days in a cool, shaded place, shaking the jar once a day.

Strain the flavored vodka into a clean bowl; whisk in the sugar until it dissolves and the mixture clears. Stir in the optional colorings and glycerine. Pour the liqueur into a clean glass bottle (or bottles), seal tightly, and allow to mature for at least 1 week before using. Store at room temperature.

NOTE: To make superfine sugar, whirl 1 1/4 cups regular granulated sugar in a food processor or in 2 batches in a blender at highest speed, until fine but not powdered. This will yield 1 1/2 cups superfine sugar.

Orange–Honey Liqueur: Replace the superfine sugar in the above recipe with 1 1/8 cups honey.

Orange Brandy: Replace the vodka in the above recipe with brandy, or use a combination of 2 cups brandy and 1 cup vodka.

Orange Rum Cordial: Replace the vodka in the above recipe with light rum; add 1 teaspoon vanilla extract; replace the superfine sugar with 1 1/4 cups granulated (sometimes called "Brownulated") light-brown sugar, whirled in a blender or food processor until fine.

RASPBERRY LIQUEUR

A delightful way to capture the flavors of summer.

MAKES 1 PINT

2 1/2 to 3 cups ripe raspberries, rinsed

2 cups (approximately) brandy

3/4 cup sugar

1/3 cup water

1 tablespoon grated lemon zest

1/2 teaspoon glycerine (optional thickener)

Lightly crush 2 cups of the berries with a fork or potato masher; place in a quart-size glass canning jar or any other quart-size glass jar that has an enamel-lined lid. Pour in enough brandy to cover the berries. Add equal portions of the remaining berries and brandy to reach the top of the jar's lip; make sure that all of the berries are covered by the brandy. Pour in just enough brandy to begin a small overflow, then tightly cap the jar and wipe the outside clean.

Label the date on the jar. Allow to steep in a cool, dark place for 2 months. (If a dark environment is not available, tape a piece of black construction paper around the jar.) Every 2 weeks, gently shake the jar to distribute the flavors.

After 2 months, gently pour the jar's contents through a regular strainer or sieve; discard the residue. Follow this by 2 strainings through slightly dampened cheesecloth. For true clarity and professional-looking results, pour the strained mixture through a large clean coffee filter placed inside a funnel or clean coffee cone; loosely cover the contents with plastic wrap, since the process may take several hours.

In a small saucepan, combine the sugar, water, and lemon zest. Bring to a boil over moderately high heat. Simmer, uncovered, for 5 minutes. Let cool to room temperature. Add the optional glycerine, if desired.

Funnel the strained brandy into a glass bottle, then funnel in the sugar syrup through a strainer, to remove the lemon zest. Cover tightly; shake to blend. Let mature at room temperature, or slightly cooler, for at least 1 month.

Raspberry Liqueur: Use vodka instead of the brandy in the above recipe.

Blackberry Brandy: Use either wild or cultivated blackberries instead of the raspberries in the above recipe.

Raspberry-Honey Brandy: Replace the sugar, water, and lemon zest in the above recipe with 2/3 cup honey blended with 1 tablespoon freshly squeezed, strained lemon juice.

ALMOND LIQUEUR

A classic liqueur that is enjoyed neat, on the rocks, or as an often used ingredient in this book. You've made an amaretto-like treat.

MAKES 3 CUPS

1 to 2 medium lemons
1 cup sugar
3/4 cup water
1 1/4 cups vodka
1 1/2 tablespoons almond extract
1/2 teaspoon vanilla extract
1/2 teaspoon glycerine (optional thickener)

Rinse and dry the lemons. Using the shredding side of a cheese grater, scrape the zest (yellow part) only off the lemons, until you have 1 tablespoon; be careful not to touch the white, bitter part.

In a small heavy saucepan, combine the lemon zest, sugar, and water. Cook over moderately high heat, stirring to mix and dissolve the sugar, until the mixture boils; lower the heat. Simmer, uncovered, until the mixture forms a syrup, about 5 minutes. Remove from the heat. Strain into a non-aluminum bowl and let cool to room temperature.

Stir the remaining ingredients into the cooled syrup; funnel into a clean wine bottle or quart-sized bottle or jar. Seal tightly.

Allow to mature in a cool, dark place for at least 1 week. Store at room temperature.

HAZELNUT LIQUEUR

This is a delicious homemade version of Frangelico liqueur.

MAKES ABOUT 1 PINT

1/2 pound hazelnuts, finely chopped
1 1/2 cups vodka
1/3 cup sugar
3 tablespoons water
1 teaspoon vanilla extract

In a glass bottle or jar, steep the chopped hazelnuts in the vodka for about 2 weeks in a cool, dark place, gently shaking the bottle every day.

Gently pour the jar's contents through a regular strainer or sieve, pressing hard on the nuts to release all their flavor. Follow this by 2 strainings through slightly dampened cheese-cloth. For true clarity and professional-looking results, pour the strained mixture through a large clean coffee filter placed inside a funnel or clean coffee cone; loosely cover the contents with plastic wrap, since the process may take several hours.

In a very small saucepan, combine the sugar and water. Bring to a boil over moderately high heat. Simmer, uncovered, for 5 minutes. Let cool to room temperature. Stir in the vanilla.

Funnel the strained hazelnut mixture into a glass bottle, then funnel in the sugar syrup. Cover tightly; shake to blend. Let mature at room temperature, or slightly cooler, for at least 3 weeks.

CRÈME DE MENTHE

As with commercially prepared varieties, the only difference between green and white crème de menthe is in the color. So the choice is up to you.

MAKES ABOUT 1 QUART

1 cup (packed) rinsed and dried fresh peppermint or spearmint leaves

3 cups vodka

2 cups sugar

1 cup water

1 teaspoon glycerine (optional thickener)

Green food coloring (optional)

In a quart-sized glass bottle or jar, steep the mint leaves in the vodka for about 10 days in a cool, dark place, shaking the bottle every day.

Gently pour the jar's contents through a regular strainer or sieve, pressing hard on the leaves to release all their flavor. Follow this by 2 strainings through slightly dampened cheese-cloth. For true clarity and professional-looking results, pour the strained mixture through a large clean coffee filter placed inside a funnel or clean coffee cone; loosely cover the contents with plastic wrap, since the process may take several hours.

In a small saucepan, combine the sugar and water. Bring to a boil over moderately high heat. Simmer, uncovered, for 5 minutes. Let cool to room temperature. Add the glycerine and food coloring, if desired.

Funnel the strained brandy into a glass bottle, then funnel in the sugar syrup. Cover tightly; shake to blend. Let mature at room temperature, or slightly cooler, for at least 2 weeks.

VANILLA CORDIAL

Vanilla's fragrant essence is a natural flavoring that is equally pleasing over ice cream or in the liqueur glass.

MAKES ABOUT 7 CUPS

3 cups water

2 cups firmly packed dark brown sugar

1 cup granulated sugar

1 vanilla bean, split lengthwise, or 1/4 to 1/2 cup vanilla extract

1 quart light rum

In a large saucepan, combine the water, dark brown and granulated sugars, and the vanilla bean, if used. Bring to a boil over moderate heat and boil for 5 minutes, stirring occasionally. Remove from the heat and let cool.

Add the rum and the vanilla extract, if used. Pour into 2 quart-sized bottles with tight-fitting covers. Let stand 2 weeks, shaking occasionally. Remove the vanilla bean, if used, before serving.

CHOCOLATE LIQUEUR

Not as thick as the professionally prepared version but delicious nonetheless. To add mocha nuances, drop 10 whole coffee beans into the steeping mixture.

MAKES 1 PINT

1/2 cup sugar
1/4 cup water
1 1/2 cups vodka
2 teaspoons chocolate extract
1/2 teaspoon glycerine (optional thickener)
10 whole coffee beans (optional)

In a medium saucepan, combine the sugar and water. Bring to a boil over moderately high heat. Simmer, uncovered, for 5 minutes. Let cool to room temperature.

Stir in the remaining ingredients until smooth. Funnel the mixture into a glass bottle; drop in the whole coffee beans, if desired. Cover tightly. Let mature for at least 2 weeks. Strain out the coffee beans, if desired.

COFFEE LIQUEUR

O ne of the all-time favorites.

MAKES ABOUT 5 CUPS

1 1/2 cups firmly packed light or dark brown sugar

1 cup granulated sugar

2 cups water

1/2 cup instant coffee powder or crystals

3 cups vodka

1 1/2 tablespoons vanilla extract

1 teaspoon glycerine (optional thickener)

10 whole coffee beans

In a heavy medium-sized saucepan, combine the brown and granulated sugars with the water. Bring to a boil over moderately high heat, stirring occasionally. Lower the heat. Simmer until the mixture forms a syrup, about 5 minutes.

Stir the coffee powder or crystals into the syrup with a whisk until they dissolve and the mixture is lump-free. Remove the pan from the heat. Let cool completely.

Stir in the remaining ingredients until smooth. Funnel the mixture into a half-gallon glass bottle; drop in the whole coffee beans. Cover tightly. Let mature for at least 2 weeks. Strain out the coffee beans, if desired.

Rum Maria: Replace the vodka in the above recipe with light or dark rum.

Brandied coffee cordial: Replace the vodka in the above recipe with brandy. Add a 3-inch stick of cinnamon along with the instant coffee and remove it before funneling.

CINNAMON SPICE LIQUEUR

This zesty liqueur is great mixed into whipped cream for topping gingerbread. Or add a nip to a mug of steaming tea.

MAKES ABOUT 1 PINT

1 3-inch piece stick cinnamon

1 tablespoon minced peeled fresh ginger

2 whole cloves

Few gratings nutmeg

1 cup vodka

1/2 cup brandy

1/2 cup sugar

1/4 cup water

In a glass bottle or jar, steep the cinnamon stick, minced ginger, cloves, and nutmeg in the vodka and brandy for about 2 weeks in a cool, dark place, gently shaking the bottle every day.

Gently pour the jar's contents through a regular strainer or sieve, pressing hard on the solids to release all of their flavor. Follow this by 2 strainings through slightly dampened cheesecloth. For true clarity and professional-looking results, pour the strained mixture through a large clean coffee filter placed inside a funnel or clean coffee cone; loosely cover the contents with plastic wrap, since the process may take several hours.

In a small saucepan, combine the sugar and water. Bring to a boil over moderately high heat. Simmer, uncovered, for 5 minutes. Let cool to room temperature.

Funnel the strained spice mixture into a glass bottle; then funnel in the sugar syrup. Cork tightly; shake to blend. Let mature at room temperature, or slightly cooler, for at least 1 week.

PIÑA COLADA CREAM LIQUEUR

A liqueur version of the tropical drink combining rum, pineapple, and coconut.

MAKES ABOUT 1 QUART

1 cup chopped fresh pineapple pieces
1/2 cup vodka
1 1/2 cups light rum, divided
1 cup canned cream of coconut
1/2 cup sweetened condensed milk
1/2 cup evaporated milk
2 teaspoons coconut extract

In a tightly closed glass jar, steep the pineapple in the vodka and 1/2 cup of the rum for 1 week. Strain, squeezing as much juice from the pineapple as possible.

Combine the pineapple liquid, the remaining 1 cup rum, and the rest of the ingredients in a pitcher. Pour the mixture, half at a time, into a blender. Cover and process on low speed until blended and smooth.

Serve the cream liqueur at once, over cracked ice or ice cubes. Or, transfer the mixture to a tightly covered container and refrigerate for up to 2 weeks. Stir just before serving.

MOCHA CREAM LIQUEUR

This creamy concoction goes together in a jiffy.

MAKES ABOUT 3 CUPS

1 can (14 ounces) sweetened condensed milk

1 cup dark rum

1 cup heavy cream

1/4 cup chocolate-flavored syrup

4 teaspoons instant espresso powder

1/2 teaspoon ground cinnamon

1/2 teaspoon vanilla extract

1/4 teaspoon coconut extract

Combine all of the ingredients in a food processor or blender. Cover and process on high speed until the mixture is well blended and smooth.

Serve the cordial at once, over cracked ice or ice cubes. Or, transfer the mixture to a tightly covered container and refrigerate for up to 2 weeks. Stir just before serving.

ILLUSTRATIONS:

COCKTAILS, SPRITZERS, AND FROZEN DRINKS

Iced Spiked Coffee • Coffee Foam

California Eggnog • Berry Good Eggnog

Just Peachy Frosted • Pink Smoothy

Frozen Fuzzy Navel • Apricot-Cherry Sour

Blue Moon • Green Goddess

Amaretto Alexander • Passionate Mimosas

White Sangria • Kir Royale

Strawberry Royale • Strawberry Kiss Cocktail

Raspberry-Red Wine Apéritif • Orange Wine Cooler

Holiday Punch • July 4th Wine Cup

ICED SPIKED COFFEE

Thick and foamy, this is a dessert in a glass. But it's also a treat accompanied by simple cookies.

MAKES 1 DRINK

3/4 cup chilled strong coffee
1/2 cup coffee ice cream
1/4 cup coffee liqueur

In the container of an electric blender, combine the coffee, ice cream, and liqueur. Cover and process until the mixture is thick, smooth, and foamy.

Pour the mixture into a tall glass and serve at once.

COFFEE FOAM

This heady drink is lightly softened with a touch of cream.

MAKES 1 DRINK

1 ounce Kahlúa, crème de cacao, or Grand Marnier
1 tablespoon heavy cream
1 teaspoon powdered sugar
1/3 cup double-strength iced coffee
1/3 cup seltzer

Place the liqueur, cream, and sugar in the bottom of a tall fluted glass.

Pour the coffee, then the seltzer, into the glass.

CALIFORNIA EGGNOG

Flavored with apricot brandy and orange liqueur, this eggnog is equally suitable served Christmas morning or with light cookies in the afternoon. Because it's made from prepared eggnog, it's a breeze to make.

MAKES 8 SERVINGS

1 quart cold prepared eggnog
1 1/2 cups apricot brandy
1/4 cup Triple Sec
Grated or ground nutmeg, for garnish

In a large pitcher, combine the eggnog, apricot brandy, and Triple Sec. Stir well to blend. Cover and refrigerate for at least 4 hours to blend flavors.

At serving time, garnish each serving with a sprinkling of nutmeg.

BERRY GOOD EGGNOG

A richly flavored, deep-hued eggnog that is sure to garner comments!

MAKES 10 SERVINGS

1 package (10 ounces) frozen raspberries in syrup, thawed
1 quart cold prepared eggnog
1 cup Chambord or other raspberry liqueur

Purée the raspberries; strain through a fine sieve to remove the seeds. Transfer the purée to a pitcher.

Stir the eggnog and liqueur into the purée. Cover and refrigerate for at least 4 hours to blend flavors.

JUST PEACHY FROSTED

The ne plus ultra peach frosted, deriving its intense flavor from three forms of the luscious fruit.

MAKES 2 TALL DRINKS

1 ripe peach

1 1/2 cups peach ice cream

1/2 cup peach schnapps

1/4 cup milk

Peel and pit the peach; then slice it directly into a blender.

Add the ice cream, peach schnapps, and milk. Cover and process until thick, smooth, and creamy. Pour into 2 chilled tall glasses and serve at once.

PINK SMOOTHY

An ice cream version of the classic Pink Squirrel, combining nutty crème de noyaux liqueur with crème de cacao.

MAKES 1 DRINK

1 ounce (2 tablespoons) crème de noyaux

1 ounce (2 tablespoons) white crème de cacao

2/3 cup vanilla ice cream

Combine the liqueurs with the ice cream in a blender. Cover and process until thick, smooth, and creamy. Pour into a chilled tall glass and serve at once.

FROZEN FUZZY NAVEL

As of this printing, the Fuzzy Navel is the most popular liqueur-based drink in the United States. This is the slushy version.

MAKES 1 DRINK

1/2 cup orange juice

1/4 cup peach schnapps

1 cup crushed ice

In a blender, combine the orange juice, peach schnapps, and crushed ice. Cover and process until thick, smooth, and creamy. Pour into a chilled tall glass and serve at once.

APRICOT-CHERRY SOUR

A little less sour, a little sweeter, than the whiskey version.

MAKES 1 DRINK

1 ounce (2 tablespoons) apricot liqueur

1/2 ounce (1 tablespoon) cherry liqueur

1 ounce (2 tablespoons) freshly squeezed lemon juice

1 teaspoon sugar

Lemon twist and maraschino cherry

In a cocktail shaker filled with ice, combine all of the ingredients except the lemon twist and maraschino cherry. Shake vigorously to mix, and chill. Strain the drink into a cocktail glass. Garnish with the lemon twist and maraschino cherry. Serve at once.

BLUE MOON

Many visitors to the Caribbean dispense with their suspicion of blue food and drink to partake of blue curaçao. This frozen drink takes advantage of the liqueur's color and its orange flavor.

MAKES 1 DRINK

1 1/2 ounces (3 tablespoons) light rum

1 ounce (2 tablespoons) blue curaçao

1 ounce (2 tablespoons) canned cream of coconut

1 ounce (2 tablespoons) freshly squeezed lime juice

1 ounce (2 tablespoons) unsweetened pineapple juice

2/3 cup crushed ice

Combine all the ingredients in a blender, cover and process until thick, smooth, and creamy. Pour into a chilled tall glass and serve at once.

GREEN GODDESS

Green Chartreuse, the herbal liqueur created by the Carthusian monks in France, goes into this unusually flavored cocktail.

MAKES 1 DRINK

1 ounce (2 tablespoons) gin

1/2 ounce (1 tablespoon) freshly squeezed lime juice

1/2 ounce (1 tablespoon) Green Chartreuse

Lime slice

In a cocktail shaker filled with ice, combine all the ingredients except the lime slice. Shake vigorously to mix, and chill. Strain the drink into a cocktail glass. Garnish with the lime slice and serve at once.

AMARETTO ALEXANDER

A creamy drink that can take the place of dessert.

MAKES 1 DRINK

1 ounce (2 tablespoons) amaretto
1 ounce (2 tablespoons) heavy cream
1 ounce (2 tablespoons) crème de cacao
Sweetened cocoa powder

In a cocktail shaker filled with ice, combine all of the ingredients except for the cocoa powder. Shake vigorously to mix and chill. Strain the drink into a cocktail glass. Sprinkle the top with the cocoa powder and serve at once.

PASSIONATE MIMOSAS

Alizé or La Grande Passion (passion fruit liqueurs) add a tropical accent to the traditional champagne drink, a nice switch at brunch.

MAKES 8 DRINKS

1 quart well-chilled freshly squeezed and strained orange juice
1/2 cup Alizé (passion fruit liqueur), chilled
1 bottle chilled champagne

Into a pitcher, pour the orange juice, then the passion fruit liqueur and the champagne. Stir just to mix, no longer (this preserves the champagne's bubbles).

WHITE SANGRIA

Refreshing with spicy food on a hot summer evening.

MAKES ABOUT 1 1/2 QUARTS

1 bottle (1 liter) chilled fruity white wine, such as a Chardonnay or Gewurztraminer

1/3 cup orange liqueur

2 cups club soda, chilled

1 orange, sliced

1 lemon, sliced

1 small cantaloupe, peeled and cut into cubes

1 cup seedless grapes, halved

In a chilled glass pitcher, combine the wine and liqueur. Stir in the soda; then add the orange and lemon slices, cantaloupe, and grapes. Serve over ice.

KIR ROYALE

Champagne replaces white wine in this ever-popular apéritif. Serve neat or on the rocks.

MAKES 1 DRINK

1 tablespoon crème de cassis for each glass

Chilled champagne (about 6 ounces per serving)

Pour crème de cassis into the bottom of each champagne glass, then fill the glasses with champagne. Serve at once.

STRAWBERRY ROYALE

Fraise des bois, wild strawberry liqueur, adds a romantic touch to all drinks.

MAKES 1 DRINK

1 tablespoon fraise des bois

Chilled champagne (about 6 ounces)

1 small strawberry, rinsed but with the hull left on

Pour the liqueur into the bottom of a champagne glass, then fill the glass with champagne. Drop the strawberry into the glass. Serve at once.

STRAWBERRY KISS COCKTAIL

Slushy blender drinks should be served with a demitasse spoon, to be savored slowly as they melt.

MAKES 1 DRINK

6 strawberries, rinsed

1/2 cup crushed ice

3/4 cup white wine

1/4 cup fraise des bois

Reserve one of the strawberries for garnish. Hull the remainder, then slice them directly into a blender. Add the wine, ice, and liqueur. Cover and process on high speed until smooth. Pour into a large stemmed glass and garnish with the reserved strawberry.

RASPBERRY-RED WINE APÉRITIF

This pre-dinner apéritif combines the berrylike flavor of a Zinfandel wine with raspberry liqueur. The liqueur serves to flavor, sweeten, and preserve the wine. Pour into decorative bottles for gift giving.

MAKES 1 QUART

1 bottle (750 ml) Zinfandel
3/4 cup raspberry or blackberry liqueur
1 3-inch strip lemon zest

Using a funnel, pour the wine into a clean 1- to 1 1/2- quart bottle; add the liqueur and lemon zest. (If you don't have a large enough bottle, divide the wine and liqueur between 2 smaller bottles; halve the zest and add a piece to each bottle.)

Seal the bottle(s) airtight with a cork. Shake to blend the contents.

Let stand at room temperature, away from direct sunlight, for 1 day. Then refrigerate for up to 3 months. At serving time, serve well chilled over ice.

ORANGE WINE COOLER

Here's a popular wine cooler that's easy to make and fresher tasting than the commercial variety.

MAKES ABOUT 4 CUPS

2 cups freshly squeezed, strained orange juice

1 1/2 cups dry white wine

1/4 cup orange liqueur

1 tablespoon freshly squeezed, strained lemon juice

Combine all the ingredients in a large pitcher or jar. Cover and refrigerate until well chilled. Stir or shake before serving.

HOLIDAY PUNCH

A colorful punch that can be made with or without the champagne.

MAKES 15 SERVINGS

1 cup crème de cassis

1/4 cup sugar

3 tablespoons freshly squeezed lemon juice

1 quart cranberry–raspberry juice

1 bottle (750 ml) champagne, chilled (optional)

1 bottle (12 ounces) seltzer or club soda, chilled

Ice mold or ice cubes (optional)

Lemon slices (optional)

In a punch bowl or large pitcher, combine the crème de cassis, sugar, and lemon juice until blended. Pour in the cranberry-raspberry juice. Cover and refrigerate until serving time, or up to 2 days.

At serving time, pour the punch into a punch bowl if the base was stored in a pitcher. Add the champagne and seltzer or club soda. Add the ice mold or ice cubes and lemon slices, if desired. Serve at once.

JULY 4TH WINE CUP

This is a variation of a recipe that appeared in Louis DeGouy's *The Cocktail Hour.*

MAKES 6 SERVINGS

Ice block
2 navel oranges
1/4 cup blueberries
1/4 cup raspberries
1 lemon
1 bottle (1 liter) white wine
1/3 cup Chambord or other raspberry liqueur

Place the ice block in a small punch bowl.

Peel and section one of the oranges; place the orange sections, blueberries, and raspberries in the punch bowl.

Grate enough lemon zest to measure 1 teaspoon. Juice the lemon and the remaining orange; add the juices and the zest to the punch bowl. Pour over the wine and the liqueur.

NOTE: The recipe can be multiplied.

COFFEES AND OTHER HOT DRINKS

Raspberry Tea   •   Café Valencia

Jamaican Coffee   •   Café St. Moritz

Creamy Irish Coffee   •   Caffè Amore

Grown-Up Cocoa   •   Mochachino

Chocolate Brûlé   •   Cherry Bomb

Hot Buttered Cider   •   Orange-Cranberry Toddy

French Glogg

RASPBERRY TEA

Raspberry liqueur turns comforting tea into another beverage altogether—still a cozy drink but at the same time something with a touch of zing.

MAKES 6 SERVINGS

6 3-inch cinnamon sticks

1 lemon, thinly sliced

1/2 pint fresh raspberries (optional)

Honey to taste (optional)

3/4 cup raspberry liqueur

4 cups freshly brewed plain or raspberry-flavored tea

Place a cinnamon stick, lemon slice and 2 or 3 raspberries, if desired, in each of 6 mugs. Add a spoonful or two of honey, if desired.

Pour 2 tablespoons liqueur into each mug. Fill the mugs with the tea, stir, and serve at once.

CAFÉ VALENCIA

The fragrance of the orange liqueur adds a lovely resonance to this subtly spiced coffee.

MAKES 1 SERVING

1 sugar cube

1 jigger (3 tablespoons) Grand Marnier or other orange liqueur

1 cup freshly brewed coffee

Orange zest twist (see Note)

1 whole clove

1 cinnamon stick

In a mug, dissolve the sugar in the liqueur. Add the coffee, the orange zest twist pierced with the clove, and the cinnamon stick. Serve at once.

NOTE: To make orange zest twist, slice a long thin spiral of the colored part only from the peel, using a swivel-bladed vegetable peeler or very sharp paring knife.

JAMAICAN COFFEE

The brown sugar-lemon juice coating infuses each sip.

MAKES 2 SERVINGS

1 *lemon wedge*

1/4 *cup firmly packed light- or dark-brown sugar plus additional for sprinkling*

1/4 *cup Tiá Maria*

2 *tablespoons orange liqueur*

2 1/2 *cups strong freshly brewed coffee*

1/3 *cup heavy cream, lightly whipped*

Orange zest slivers, for garnish (optional)

Rub the cut side of the lemon wedge around the rim of 2 heatproof glasses or mugs. Spread out the brown sugar on a plate. Dip the rims into the sugar to coat them.

Spoon 2 tablespoons of the Tiá Maria and 1 tablespoon of the orange liqueur into each of the glasses. Pour the coffee over the liqueurs.

Float the whipped cream over the coffee. Sprinkle with additional brown sugar and scatter orange zest slivers over the top, if desired. Serve at once.

CAFÉ ST. MORITZ

Peppermint and chocolate go as well together in coffee as they do in desserts and candy. This bracing example is wonderful after cold-weather sports.

MAKES 1 SERVING

1 cup freshly brewed coffee

1/2 jigger (1 1/2 tablespoons) white crème de menthe

1/2 jigger (1 1/2 tablespoons) white or brown crème de cacao

1 tablespoon whipped cream

1 teaspoon green crème de cacao, for garnish (optional)

Chocolate shavings, for garnish (optional; see Note)

In a mug, combine the coffee with the white crème de menthe and crème de cacao.

Top with the whipped cream. If desired, drizzle the green crème de cacao and chocolate shavings over the top. Serve at once.

NOTE: To make chocolate shavings, hold a sharp knife almost parallel to the surface of a piece of solid chocolate; carefully push the blade away from you, carving off long, thin curls.

CREAMY IRISH COFFEE

Instead of Irish whiskey, this simple concoction uses Irish cream liqueur. Because the liqueur is rich on its own, the whipped cream topping is optional.

MAKES 2 SERVINGS

1/3 cup Irish cream liqueur

1 1/2 cups freshly brewed coffee

1/4 cup heavy cream, slightly sweetened and whipped (optional)

Divide the liqueur and coffee between 2 mugs. Top with poufs of whipped cream if desired. Serve at once.

CAFFÈ AMORE

Sambuca is a sybaritic blend of licorice and wild elderberry, often served neat, with 3 roasted coffee beans.

MAKES 2 SERVINGS

1/2 cup heavy cream

2 teaspoons sugar

1/3 cup Sambuca or anisette

1 1/2 cups freshly brewed strong coffee

6 perfect roasted coffee beans or chocolate coffee beans

In a small bowl, beat the cream and the sugar until the cream holds firm peaks. Transfer the cream to a pastry bag fitted with a medium star tip.

Divide the Sambuca and the coffee between 2 mugs.

Pipe the cream in a spiral over the coffee. Garnish each mug with 3 coffee beans. Serve at once.

GROWN-UP COCOA

A nursery beverage grows up in this drink laced with liqueur and vodka.

MAKES 1 SERVING

1 cup prepared cocoa

1 jigger (3 tablespoons) peppermint schnapps

1/2 jigger (1 1/2 tablespoons) vodka

2 tablespoons whipped cream

Chocolate shavings (optional; see Note, page 56), optional

1 small peppermint stick (optional)

In a mug, combine the cocoa, schnapps, and vodka.

Top with the whipped cream. If desired sprinkle the chocolate shavings over the top and insert the peppermint stick into the cream.

MOCHACHINO

A cross between a rich hot chocolate and coffee.

MAKES 4 SERVINGS

1 square (1 ounce) semisweet chocolate, chopped

2 tablespoons sugar

3/4 cup boiling water

1 3/4 cups freshly brewed coffee

1 cup light cream, scalded

2 tablespoons crème de cacao

2 tablespoons coffee liqueur

1 tablespoon sugar mixed with 1 teaspoon unsweetened cocoa powder, for garnish (optional)

In the top of a double boiler set over hot water (or in a medium very heavy saucepan), combine the chocolate and sugar. Heat, stirring often, until the chocolate melts. Slowly beat in the water with a wire whisk. Continue heating, stirring often, for 3 minutes longer.

Stir in the coffee and scalded cream until blended. Remove the pan from the heat. Stir in the crème de cacao and the coffee liqueur.

Divide the mixture among 4 heated mugs. Sprinkle with the sugar and cocoa mixture, if desired and serve immediately.

CHOCOLATE BRÛLÉ

Liqueur Brûlé is an evocative blend of caramel and cognac, a romantic addition to a cup of cocoa.

MAKES 1 DRINK

1/4 cup Liqueur Brûlé
3/4 cup prepared cocoa
Cinnamon stick
Whipped cream, for garnish

Combine the liqueur and cocoa in a mug. Stir several times with the cinnamon stick. Top with a dollop of whipped cream and serve at once.

CHERRY BOMB

This potent flambéed drink combines the flavors of a chocolate-covered cherry.

MAKES 2 DRINKS

1/4 cup heavy cream

1/3 cup dark rum

3 tablespoons crème de cacao

3 tablespoons cherry liqueur or cherry brandy

2 teaspoons sugar

Chocolate shavings (page 56) and/or liqueur-soaked cherries (optional), for garnish

In a small bowl, very lightly whip the cream until it is thickened but still of pouring consistency. Set aside.

In a small saucepan, combine the rum, crème de cacao, cherry liqueur, and sugar.

Heat the mixture over moderately low heat, just until it is hot. Remove the pan from the heat.

With a very long match, ignite the hot mixture, shaking the pan until the flames subside.

Divide the hot mixture between 2 sturdy stemmed glasses (a metal spoon inserted in the glasses before they are filled will prevent breakage).

Pour the whipped cream over the back of a spoon into each of the glasses. Garnish with the optional chocolate curls and/or cherries. Serve at once.

HOT BUTTERED CIDER

Garnish each serving with a cinnamon stick for fragrant stirring.

MAKES 6 SERVINGS

1 quart apple cider, preferably freshly pressed

1/4 cup light corn syrup

2 tablespoons unsalted butter

2 cinnamon sticks

3 whole cloves

2 lemon slices

6 ounces apple liqueur

In a large saucepan, combine the cider, corn syrup, butter, cinnamon sticks, cloves, and lemon slices.

Heat over a moderate flame until the cider is hot and the butter is melted. Remove from the heat.

While the cider is heating, pour 1 ounce of liqueur into each of 6 mugs or heatproof glasses. Pour the hot cider into the mugs and serve at once.

ORANGE-CRANBERRY TODDY

Serve this hot drink as an alternative to tea for winter entertaining.

MAKES 8 SERVINGS

6 cups orange juice, preferably freshly squeezed

2 cups cranberry juice cocktail

1/4 cup sugar

1 stick cinnamon

8 whole cloves

1 cup cranberry and/or orange liqueur

2 navel oranges, sliced, for garnish

In a medium saucepan, combine the orange juice, cranberry juice cocktail, sugar, cinnamon, and cloves. Bring to a boil over moderate heat. Remove from the heat.

Stir in the cranberry and/or orange liqueur.

Divide the toddy among 8 mugs or heatproof glasses. Serve at once with an orange slice on top.

FRENCH GLOGG

The traditional Swedish hot wine cup with an orange accent.

MAKES 12 SERVINGS

2 bottles (1 liter each) Burgundy or other
   hearty red wine

1 cup sugar

6 whole cardamom seeds

6 whole cloves

4 cinnamon sticks

Zest of 2 navel oranges

2 cups Curaçao or other orange liqueur

1 cup golden raisins

1/2 cup sliced blanched almonds

Pour the wine into a large pot. Add the sugar, cardamom, cloves, cinnamon, and orange zest.

Place the wine over low heat until it just starts to simmer but does not come to a boil. The sugar should be dissolved.

Add the curaçao to the wine. Heat, then light with a long match.

When the flames subside, strain the hot mixture into a fondue pot over a candle warmer, if desired (or, for more casual service, ladle directly from the pot set over very low heat); add the raisins.

Ladle the glogg into mugs or heatproof cups, making sure to add a few raisins to each serving. Sprinkle some almonds into each mug as it is served.

CAKES, PIES, AND TARTS

Cranberry Sacher Torte • Chambord Linzer Torte

Banana Coffee Cake • Grand Marnier Pound Cake

Chocolate Kahlúa Cake • Bountiful Chocolate Cake

Applesauce Cake • Marble Cheesecake

Amaretto Fudge Cheesecake • Little Almond Amaretto Loaves

Apple and Kumquat Pie • Fruit Compote Pie

Pumpkin Praline Pie • Deep-Dish Double Berry Pie

Banana Cream Pie • Macadamia Cream Pie

Bailey's Irish Cream Brownie Pie • Lemon Angel Pie

Dried Cherry and Apple Turnovers

Prune-Apricot Foldovers

CRANBERRY SACHER TORTE

This is a variation of the classic Viennese cake. Here, cranberry pieces punctuate the cake batter, which is topped with cranberry sauce, then enrobed in a deep chocolate glaze.

MAKES ONE 9-INCH CAKE, 10 TO 12 PORTIONS

Cake:

    8 ounces semisweet chocolate, chopped

    1 cup (2 sticks) unsalted butter, softened

  2/3 cup sugar

    7 extra-large eggs, separated

    1 cup all-purpose flour

    1 cup fresh or frozen raw cranberries, chopped (see Note)

  1/4 teaspoon salt

Cranberry topping:

  1/2 cup whole-berry cranberry sauce

    1 tablespoon cranberry liqueur or light or dark rum

Chocolate glaze:

    8 ounces semisweet chocolate, chopped

  1/3 cup sugar

  1/3 cup water

    5 tablespoons unsalted butter

Cake:

Preheat the oven to 350 degrees. Butter a 9-inch springform pan; line the bottom with wax paper cut to fit; butter the paper, dust with flour, tapping out the excess. Set aside while preparing the batter.

Melt the chocolate in the top of a double boiler set over simmering water (or melt the chocolate in the microwave oven). Remove from the heat; let cool slightly.

Meanwhile, cream the butter in a large bowl with the electric mixer on high speed; slowly beat in the sugar, then beat in the egg yolks, half at a time, beating well after each addition. Turn the mixer speed to low; beat in the melted chocolate until blended. Beat in the flour just until it is absorbed. Fold in the chopped cranberries.

In a separate small bowl with clean beaters, beat the egg whites and salt until soft peaks form. Stir about one fourth of the egg whites into the chocolate mixture. Fold in the remainder, about one fourth at a time. Quickly scrape the batter into the prepared pan, gently smoothing the top.

Bake for 40 to 45 minutes, or until the top is firm and springs back when lightly pressed with a fingertip. Let the cake cool in the pan on a wire rack for 10 minutes. Carefully loosen the side of the cake from the pan; remove the side of the pan; invert the cake onto the rack, remove the pan bottom and wax paper, then turn right side up. Let the cake cool completely on the rack.

Cranberry topping:

Combine the cranberry sauce and rum in a small saucepan; bring to a boil over moderate heat. Spoon the hot sauce over the cake; carefully spread it over the top in an even layer, crushing any large pieces of cranberry.

Chocolate glaze:

Place the chocolate, sugar, and water in the top of a double boiler. Place over, not in, simmering water. Heat, stirring occasionally, until the chocolate melts and the mixture is smooth. Remove from the hot water. Add the butter and stir until it melts. Let the glaze stand at room temperature, stirring occasionally, for about 30 minutes, or until it starts to thicken.

Put a large piece of wax paper under the cake on the wire rack. Slowly pour the glaze over the top of the cake so some runs over the sides. Let stand for at least 1 hour, until the glaze sets. If the glaze is still soft, place the cake in the refrigerator. If desired, decorate the cake with sugar-frosted cranberries and serve with rum-flavored whipped cream.

NOTE: The cranberries are easy to chop in the food processor; for best results, process with on-off pulses, until the cranberries are chopped. If you have raw cranberries in the freezer, chop them when they are still frozen.

CHAMBORD LINZER TORTE

The tart base has a lovely nutty flavor, redolent of spices. It is filled with raspberry preserves, then covered with a latticework of dough.

MAKES ONE 9-INCH TART, 8 TO 10 SERVINGS

Dough:

2 1/2 cups all-purpose flour

3 tablespoons unsweetened cocoa powder

2 teaspoons ground cinnamon

1 teaspoon baking powder

1/4 teaspoon salt

1 cup ground almonds

1 cup (2 sticks) unsalted butter, softened

1 cup sugar

1 egg

2 egg yolks

1 cup high-quality raspberry preserves

2 tablespoons Chambord or other raspberry liqueur

1 egg, lightly beaten, for the glaze

Dough:

Into a small bowl, sift together the flour, cocoa, cinnamon, baking powder, and salt. Stir in the almonds. Set aside.

In a large bowl with an electric mixer on high speed, beat the butter until light. Gradually beat in the sugar and continue beating until light and fluffy. Add the egg and egg yolks.

Turn the mixer speed to low. Add the flour mixture all at once and beat just until it is absorbed. The dough will be quite soft. Do not worry. Transfer the dough to a piece of wax paper or plastic wrap. Wrap and chill until firm, at least 4 hours.

Assembling the tart:

When ready to bake, preheat the oven to 350 degrees.

In a small bowl, combine the raspberry preserves and liqueur; set aside.

Roll out half the dough to 1/4-inch thickness on a well-floured surface. Cut into 12-inch circle. Carefully transfer the dough to a 9- or 10-inch tart pan with a removable bottom. If dough breaks, pinch it smooth. Refrigerate the dough-lined tart pan for 15 minutes.

Meanwhile, roll out the second piece of dough to a 12- by 4-inch rectangle. With a sharp knife, cut 10 lengthwise strips.

Remove the tart pan from the refrigerator. Gently spread the preserves over the bottom.

Arrange the dough strips in a lattice pattern over the top; trim the edges of the strips flush with the bottom of the dough, then trim the overhang of the dough to 1-inch overhang all around. Fold the overhang over the strips, pinching to seal. Gently brush the beaten egg over the strips.

Bake the tart until the crust is golden brown and firm, and the preserves bubble up, about 45 minutes. Cool completely before serving.

BANANA COFFEE CAKE

Accented with coconut and nuts, this makes a perfect brunch or teatime cake. Serve simply dusted with the powdered sugar or use one of the two glaze recipes; the first produces a very moist, saucelike topping while the second hardens to a white topping.

MAKES ONE 12-CUP TUBE CAKE, 10 TO 12 SERVINGS

Cake:

   3 cups all-purpose flour

   2 teaspoons baking powder

   1 teaspoon baking soda

1/2 teaspoon salt

   1 teaspoon ground cinnamon

Large pinch ground nutmeg

1 1/2 cups mashed ripe banana (about 3
      medium-large)

1/2 cup banana liqueur

1/3 cup sour cream

   1 teaspoon vanilla extract

   1 cup (2 sticks) unsalted butter, softened

   1 cup sugar

   4 extra-large eggs

3/4 cup flaked coconut

3/4 cup chopped walnuts or pecans

1/4 cup banana liqueur, for brushing on
      just-baked cake

Glaze I (optional):

   1 cup sifted powdered sugar

1/4 cup mashed banana (about 1/2 medium)

   2 tablespoons unsalted butter, softened

   1 tablespoon banana liqueur

   1 teaspoon lemon juice

OR:

Glaze II (optional):

3/4 cup sifted powdered sugar

   2 tablespoons unsalted butter, softened

   2 tablespoons banana liqueur

OR:

Sifted powdered sugar, for dusting on top of
      the cake

Cake:

Preheat the oven to 350 degrees. Butter a 12-cup tube pan; set aside.

Sift together the flour, baking powder, baking soda, salt, cinnamon, and nutmeg; set aside. In a small bowl, combine the banana, liqueur, sour cream, and vanilla extract; set aside.

In a large bowl with the electric mixer on high speed, beat the butter until it is light. Gradually beat in the sugar and continue beating until the mixture is very light and fluffy, about 5 minutes. Lower the mixer speed to low. Beat in the eggs, 2 at a time, beating just until blended.

Alternately beat in the flour and banana mixtures in about 3 additions, beginning and ending with the flour. Beat just until blended. Turn off the mixer. Stir in the coconut and nuts. Spread the batter in the prepared pan, smoothing the top.

Bake in the preheated oven until the cake is golden brown and pulls away from the side of the pan and a skewer inserted in the cake, halfway between the tube and the side comes out clean, about 1 hour to 1 hour and 10 minutes. Loosely cover the cake with aluminum foil during the baking if the top is getting too dark. Remove the cake from the oven; let cool in the pan on a wire rack for 10 minutes.

Carefully invert the cake from the pan onto a cake plate; remove the pan. Brush the cake all over with the 1/4 cup liqueur. Let cool. Drizzle with either of the optional glazes or dust the top of the cake with the sifted powdered sugar.

Glazes I and II:

If desired, while the cake cools, combine all the glaze ingredients in a small bowl until well blended. When the cake is lukewarm, spoon the glaze over the top. Let the cake cool completely.

GRAND MARNIER POUND CAKE

A rich pound cake that is delicious served simply with liqueur-flavored whipped cream and berries; or you may want to try it with scoops of orange sherbet and vanilla ice cream. Don't be alarmed by the unconventional mixing method.

MAKES ONE 10-INCH TUBE CAKE, ABOUT 12 PORTIONS

Cake:

- 1 cup (2 sticks) unsalted butter, softened
- 1 2/3 cups sugar
- 2 cups all-purpose unbleached flour
- 1 teaspoon baking powder
- 1/4 teaspoon salt
- 1/4 cup Grand Marnier
- 1 tablespoon grated orange zest
- 5 eggs

Glaze:

- 1/4 cup freshly squeezed orange juice
- 1/4 cup Grand Marnier
- 1/4 cup sugar

Cake:

Preheat the oven to 350 degrees. Generously butter a 10-inch (9-cup) fluted tube pan; then sprinkle it with flour, tapping out the excess. Set aside.

In a large bowl with the electric mixer on high speed, beat the butter until creamy. Gradually beat in the sugar and continue beating until the mixture is light and fluffy. Turn the mixer speed to low.

Sift in the flour, baking powder, and salt. Beat just until the flour is absorbed. Beat in the Grand Marnier and orange zest. Beat in the eggs, one at a time, beating well after each addition.

Spread the batter in the prepared pan, smoothing the top even.

Bake until the cake shrinks from the side of the pan and a skewer inserted in the middle comes out clean, about 1 hour and 5 minutes. Let stand in the pan on a wire rack for 10 minutes, then carefully unmold the cake onto a second rack placed over a piece of wax paper or aluminum foil.

Glaze:

Meanwhile, combine the orange juice, Grand Marnier, and sugar in a small saucepan. Bring to a boil over moderate heat. Lower the heat and simmer until the mixture forms a light syrup, about 5 minutes. Then brush the syrup all over the warm cake. When the cake is cool, transfer it to a serving plate.

CHOCOLATE KAHLÚA CAKE

A handsome bundt cake is split into three tiers, then reassembled with a rich Kahlúa-fortified buttercream.

MAKES ONE 12-INCH CAKE, 16 SERVINGS

Cake:

2 2/3 cups all-purpose flour

   2 teaspoons baking powder

   1 teaspoon baking soda

1/2 teaspoon salt

   1 cup (2 sticks) unsalted butter, softened

   2 cups firmly packed light and/or dark brown sugar

   1 teaspoon vanilla extract

   3 extra-large eggs

   1 cup unsweetened cocoa powder

3/4 cup milk

3/4 cup cold strong coffee

1/4 cup Kahlúa

Filling:

1/2 cup (1 stick) unsalted butter, softened

   2 bars (3 ounces each) bittersweet chocolate, chopped, melted, and cooled

1/4 cup Kahlúa

   1 tablespoon instant espresso powder, dissolved in 1 teaspoon hot water and cooled

1/4 cup powdered sugar, sifted if lumpy

1/4 cup Kahlúa, for sprinkling on the layers

Glaze:

1 1/2 cups sifted powdered sugar

   2 tablespoons cold strong coffee

   2 tablespoons Kahlúa

Cake:

Preheat the oven to 350 degrees. Butter a 10-inch (12-cup) fluted tube pan; then flour it, shaking out the excess. Set the pan aside.

Sift together the flour, baking powder, baking soda, and salt onto a piece of wax paper.

In a medium or large bowl with the electric mixer at high speed, beat the butter until soft. Gradually beat in the sugar and continue beating until the mixture is light and fluffy. Lower the mixer speed to medium-low. Add the vanilla, then the eggs, one at a time, beating well after each addition. Beat in the cocoa powder.

Lower the mixer speed to low. Alternately in about 3 additions, beat in the sifted dry ingredients and the milk, coffee, and Kahlúa, beginning and ending with the dry ingredients. Pour the batter into the prepared pan, smoothing the top if necessary.

Bake in the preheated oven until a skewer inserted halfway between the tube and the side of the pan comes out clean, about 1 hour. Let the cake stand in the pan on a wire rack for 10 minutes, then carefully invert it onto the rack and let it cool completely.

Filling:

In a small bowl with the electric mixer at high speed, beat together the butter, melted and cooled chocolate, Kahlúa, and espresso dissolved in hot water. Reduce the mixer speed to low; gradually beat in the powdered sugar. Refrigerate the filling to firm it up for spreading, usually 10 to 20 minutes.

Slice the cake horizontally into 3 layers, using a serrated knife. Place one of the layers, cut-side up, on a large plate. Brush with half of the Kahlúa, then carefully spread half of the filling in an even layer over the top. Repeat with another cake layer and the remaining Kahlúa and frosting. Top with the remaining layer, lightly pressing down on the cake to adhere the layers. Refrigerate the cake while preparing the glaze.

Glaze:

In a small bowl, blend together the sugar, coffee, and Kahlúa until smooth and well blended.

Drizzle the cake with the glaze. Refrigerate the cake for up to 1 day.

BOUNTIFUL CHOCOLATE CAKE

Filled with chopped prunes and almonds, this is a high and handsome cake befitting a birthday or other celebration.

MAKES ONE 9-INCH CAKE, 12 SERVINGS

Cake layers:

- 1 cup whole unblanched almonds
- 5 squares (1 ounce each) unsweetened chocolate
- 1 cup blackberry brandy
- 1 package (12 ounces) pitted prunes
- 1 2/3 cups all-purpose flour
- 1 teaspoon baking soda
- 1/2 teaspoon salt
- 1/2 cup (1 stick) unsalted butter, softened
- 1 cup granulated sugar
- 1 cup firmly packed light brown sugar
- 4 eggs, separated
- 1 teaspoon vanilla extract
- 1 cup buttermilk

Chocolate frosting:

- 1 bar (3 ounces) semisweet or bittersweet chocolate
- 1 bar (3 ounces) milk chocolate
- 1/4 cup sugar
- 1/3 cup water
- 2 teaspoons instant espresso powder
- 4 egg yolks
- 3 tablespoons blackberry brandy
- 1 cup (2 sticks) unsalted butter, cut up and softened

Cake layers:

Preheat the oven to 350 degrees. While the oven is preheating, toast the almonds in a single layer on a baking sheet for 10 to 15 minutes. Butter two 9-inch baking pans; flour the pans, tapping out the excess. Set aside.

In a small heavy saucepan over low heat, melt the chocolate in the liqueur, stirring occasionally. Remove from the heat; let cool completely.

In a food processor, place the almonds, prunes, and 1/3 cup of the flour. Cover and pulse-chop just until coarsely chopped. Set aside.

Onto a sheet of wax paper, sift together the remaining flour, baking soda, and salt. Set aside.

In a large bowl with the electric mixer on high speed, beat the butter until it is light. Gradually beat in all but 1/4 cup of the granulated sugar, then the brown sugar, until light and fluffy. Reduce the mixer speed to medium. Beat in the egg yolks, one at a time; then beat in the vanilla and the chocolate mixture.

In 3 additions, alternately beat in the sifted flour mixture and the buttermilk, beginning and ending with the flour and beating just until combined.

Thoroughly wash and dry the beaters. In a small bowl with the mixer on high speed, beat the egg whites until foamy white. Gradually beat in the remaining 1/4 cup granulated sugar, 1 tablespoon at a time, then continue beating until the egg whites form stiff, not dry, peaks.

Stir about 1/2 cup of the beaten egg whites into the chocolate batter, to lighten it, then fold in the remainder. Fold in the chopped prunes and nuts. Divide the batter between the prepared pans, smoothing the tops.

Bake the cake layers until the tops spring back when lightly pressed with a fingertip and a skewer inserted in the center comes out clean, about 40 to 45 minutes.

Cool the cake layers in the pans on wire racks for 15 minutes. Then gently loosen them from the sides of the pans and invert them onto the racks; turn right side up. Cool completely.

Chocolate frosting:

While the cake layers are cooling, in a small heavy saucepan over very low heat, melt both of the chocolates bars. Remove from the heat.

In a second small saucepan, combine the sugar, water, and coffee. Bring to a boil, stirring once or twice; continue simmering until the sugar dissolves. Remove the syrup from the heat.

In a small bowl with the electric mixer on high speed, beat the egg yolks until thick and lemon colored. Reduce the mixer speed to medium-low. Gradually beat in the hot syrup, then the melted chocolate and the blackberry brandy.

Beat in the butter, bit by bit, beating after each addition to incorporate it. If the frosting is too thin to spread, chill it for 15 to 30 minutes.

Fill and frost the cake layers with the frosting.

APPLESAUCE CAKE

This is a sturdy coffee cake with autumnal flavors. Serve it with hot cinnamon tea. If you cannot obtain apple liqueur, substitute orange liqueur or Bénédictine and brandy.

MAKES ONE 10-INCH TUBE CAKE, 16 SERVINGS

Cake:

        2 cups all-purpose flour

1 1/3 cups whole-wheat flour

        2 teaspoons ground cinnamon

        2 teaspoons baking powder

        1 teaspoon baking soda

1/2 teaspoon salt

        2 cups natural-style (unsweetened) applesauce

1/4 cup apple liqueur

        1 cup (2 sticks) unsalted butter, softened

        2 cups firmly packed light-brown sugar

        3 eggs

        1 cup raisins

        1 cup chopped pitted dates

        1 cup chopped walnuts

Cream cheese icing:

1/2 cup (1 stick) unsalted butter, softened

        4 ounces cream cheese, softened

Grated zest of 1 navel orange

        3 cups powdered sugar

        2 tablespoons apple liqueur

Cake:

Preheat the oven to 350 degrees. Butter a 10-inch (16-cup) tube cake pan; flour the pan, tapping out the excess. Set aside.

Onto a sheet of wax paper, sift together the all-purpose and whole-wheat flours, cinnamon, baking powder, baking soda, and salt. In a small bowl, stir the apple liqueur into the applesauce. Set the sifted dry ingredients and the applesauce aside.

In a large bowl with the electric mixer on high speed, cream the butter until light. Gradually add the brown sugar and continue beating until the mixture is very light and fluffy. Reduce the mixer speed to medium. Add the eggs, one at a time, beating well after each addition.

Reduce the mixer speed to slow. In 3 additions, alternately beat in the sifted dry ingredients and the applesauce, beginning and ending with the dry ingredients and beating only until combined. Turn off the mixer and stir in the raisins, dates, and walnuts.

Spread the batter in the prepared pan, smoothing the top even.

Bake the cake until a skewer inserted halfway between the side of the pan and the tube comes out clean, about 1 hour.

Cool the cake in the pan on a wire rack for 15 minutes. Carefully loosen the cake from the side of the pan and the tube; invert onto the rack. Turn right side up. Cool completely.

Cream cheese icing:

In a medium or large bowl with the electric mixer on high speed, beat together the butter and the cream cheese until light. Beat in the orange zest.

Reduce the mixer speed to medium. Gradually add the powdered sugar, alternately with the liqueur, beating until the frosting is smooth and creamy. Adjust the consistency, if necessary, by adding more powdered sugar or more liqueur.

Smooth the icing over the top and sides of the completely cooled cake.

MARBLE CHEESECAKE

Orange and chocolate complement each other beautifully in this dessert. If you like cheesecake with a soft, almost mousselike consistency, serve this cooled but unrefrigerated. Or refrigerate it for a firmer texture.

MAKES ONE 9-INCH CAKE, 15 SERVINGS

1 package (8 1/2 ounces) chocolate wafers

3/8 cup (3/4 stick) unsalted butter, melted

2 bars (3 ounces each) bittersweet chocolate, finely chopped

1/3 cup brewed coffee

2 pounds cream cheese, softened

1 cup sugar

4 eggs, at room temperature

1 cup plain yogurt

2 tablespoons Grand Marnier or other orange-flavored liqueur

1 teaspoon vanilla extract

1/4 cup all-purpose flour

1/4 teaspoon salt

Grated zest of 1 navel orange (1 tablespoon)

Preheat the oven to 325 degrees. Butter the side only of a 9-inch springform pan. Wrap the outside of the pan with aluminum foil. Set the pan aside.

In a food processor, pulverize the chocolate wafers. Transfer the crumbs to a small bowl and toss with the melted butter until evenly moistened. Press the buttered crumbs evenly over the bottom and up the side of the springform pan. (An easy way to do this is to hold the pan at a 45-degree angle from the work surface; patting the crumbs against the side of the pan, rotate the pan.)

In a small heavy saucepan, melt the chocolate in the coffee over low heat. Beat with a wire whisk until smooth. Set aside.

In the large bowl of an electric mixer, beat the cream cheese at high speed until creamy and smooth. Gradually beat in the sugar, scraping the beaters and the side of the bowl to make sure there are no lumps. Beat in the eggs, one at a time, until each is incorporated. Beat in the yogurt, Grand Marnier, and vanilla. In a cup, stir together the flour and the salt.

Lower the mixer speed to slow and beat in the flour.

Remove 1 1/2 cups of the batter to a small bowl; stir in the melted chocolate. Stir the orange zest into the remaining batter.

Pour the orange batter into the prepared pan. Spoon 8 dollops of the chocolate batter in a circle over the orange batter; place 1 more dollop in the center. With a table knife, carefully swirl the two batters, to marbleize; do not overmix the batters or they will lose their marbled appearance. With your finger, gently push any crumbs that are higher than the batter around the edge of the pan (this creates a crumb border around the top).

Bake the cheesecake in the preheated oven until it is firm around the edge but still quite wobbly in the center, about 1 hour. Do not overbake the cheesecake, or it will lose its creamy consistency. Cool the cheesecake in the pan on a wire rack. Gently release the side of the pan. Transfer the cake on its base onto a cake plate. Serve at room temperature or refrigerate for a firmer consistency.

AMARETTO FUDGE CHEESECAKE

An ultra-rich cheesecake to be served in thin slivers. Decorate with toasted sliced almonds and chocolate curls, if desired.

MAKES ONE 9-INCH CHEESECAKE, 15 SERVINGS

Crust:

1 package (8 1/2 ounces) chocolate wafers

3/8 cup (3/4 stick) unsalted butter, melted

Filling:

8 ounces semisweet chocolate, chopped

2 squares (1 ounce each) unsweetened chocolate, chopped

3 packages (8 ounces each) cream cheese, softened

2/3 cup sugar

1 pint sour cream

1/4 cup amaretto

5 eggs

Few drops almond extract

1/3 cup all-purpose flour

Preheat the oven to 325 degrees.

Crust:

In a food processor, pulverize the chocolate wafer. Combine them and the melted butter in a small bowl until well blended. Butter the sides of a 9-inch springform pan; press the cookie crumbs onto the bottom and three quarters of the way up the sides of the pan; set aside.

Filling:

In the top of a double boiler over simmering water, melt the semisweet and unsweetened chocolates (or melt in the microwave oven in a medium bowl). Set aside.

In a large bowl with the electric mixer on high speed; beat the cream cheese until light; gradually beat in the sugar, then the melted chocolate, sour cream, amaretto, eggs, and almond extract. Reduce the mixer speed to low. Sift the flour over the top of the bowl and beat in. Then pour the filling into the crumb-lined pan.

Finishing the cheesecake:

Bake the cheesecake for 1 hour and 15 minutes, or until the filling is firm around the edge but still jiggly in the center. Let it cool on a wire rack, then refrigerate for at least 4 hours, or until chilled.

Carefully remove the side of the pan and transfer the cake to a serving plate. Cut thin slices.

LITTLE ALMOND–AMARETTO LOAVES

Serve slices of this extra-moist loaf sandwiched with raspberry jam for teatime, brunch, or any time you're in the mood.

MAKES 5 SMALL LOAVES

1/2 cup (1 stick) unsalted butter, softened

1 can (8 ounces) almond paste

1 1/3 cups sugar, plus additional for sprinkling

3 eggs

2 cups all-purpose flour

1 teaspoon baking powder

Pinch salt

1/2 cup amaretto, plus additional for brushing on the cakes

1/2 cup milk

1/4 cup sliced blanched almonds

Preheat the oven to 350 degrees. Butter five 5 by 3-inch loaf pans; flour the pans, tapping out the excess flour. Set aside.

In a large or medium bowl with the electric mixer on high speed; cream the butter and almond paste until smooth. Gradually beat in the sugar and then the eggs, one at a time.

In a small bowl, stir together the flour, baking powder, and salt. Reducing the mixer speed to low, beat in the flour alternately with the amaretto and milk, beginning and ending with the flour and beating just until incorporated.

Spread the batter in the pans. Sprinkle the tops with the almonds and additional sugar.

Bake the loaves for 40 to 45 minutes, or until the tops are golden brown and a skewer inserted in the center comes out clean. Cool in the pans on wire racks for 10 minutes. Carefully loosen around the sides with a sharp knife; invert the loaves onto the racks and then turn them right side up. Brush with additional amaretto. Cool completely.

APPLE AND KUMQUAT PIE

Fresh kumquats have a fresh tart flavor that adds a piquant boost to this fruit-filled pie. If you are unable to find them, use prepared kumquats that have been rinsed and patted dry, and omit the sugar.

MAKES ONE 9-INCH PIE, 8 SERVINGS

Filling:

- 1/2 pound fresh kumquats, halved, pitted, and chopped OR: 1 jar (8 ounces) kumquats, drained, rinsed, and patted dry, pitted and chopped
- 2 cups golden raisins
- 1/2 cup Grand Marnier or other orange liqueur
- 1/2 cup dark rum
- Grated zest of 1 navel orange
- 2 tart green apples, such as Granny Smith or Greening
- 1/4 cup sugar (omit if using prepared kumquats)
- 1/2 cup orange juice
- 2 tablespoons cornstarch
- 2 cups chopped pecans

Crust:

- 2 1/2 cups all-purpose flour
- 1/3 cup sugar
- Pinch salt
- 3/4 cup (1 1/2 sticks) frozen unsalted butter, cut into 1/2-inch pieces
- 5 tablespoons ice water
- 1 egg
- 1 tablespoon water

Filling:

Combine the kumquats, raisins, Grand Marnier, rum, and orange zest in a medium saucepan; toss to blend together; cover with plastic wrap. Let stand for at least 4 hours, or overnight.

Crust:

Meanwhile, place the flour, sugar, and salt in a food processor; toss in the butter pieces. Cover and process with on-and-off pulses until the mixture resembles coarse crumbs.

With the motor running, pour the ice water through the feed tube; continue pulse-processing until the dough forms a ball, but no more than 30 seconds. Remove the dough from the processor. If the mixture does not hold together, sprinkle an additional tablespoon of ice water over the top. Flatten the dough into a disk and wrap it in plastic wrap. Refrigerate the dough for 3 hours.

Filling:

Remove the plastic wrap from the saucepan. Halve, core, peel, and chop the apples; stir them into the kumquat mixture along with the sugar (if using), orange juice, and cornstarch. Bring to a simmer over medium heat, stirring constantly; continue cooking until the mixture thickens and bubbles. Remove the saucepan from the heat and cool the mixture completely.

Assembling the pie:

Preheat the oven to 375 degrees. Roll out half the dough on a lightly floured surface to an 11-inch circle. Press the circle into a 9-inch pie pan, trimming the overhang to 1 inch.

Stir the pecans into the cooled filling; then spread the filling over the bottom crust.

Roll out the remaining dough to a 1/8-inch thickness; cut it into 1/2-inch wide strips. Arrange the strips in a lattice pattern over the filling and trim the strips even with the overhang of the bottom crust. Fold the bottom edge over the strips; crimp all around.

Beat together the egg and water; brush the egg mixture over the pastry lattice.

Bake the pie in the preheated oven until the filling bubbles up and the pastry is golden brown, about 45 minutes.

FRUIT COMPOTE PIE

Crisp crumbs top a tangy sour cream and dried fruit filling.

MAKES ONE 9-INCH PIE, 6 SERVINGS

*Pastry dough for a single 9-inch pie crust
(page 94)*

Fruit compote:

- *1 cup dried apricots*
- *1 cup dried peaches and/or apples*
- *1 can (6 ounces) apricot or peach nectar*
- *1/4 cup apricot or peach liqueur*
- *2 tablespoons dried cranberries, or cherries, or golden raisins*

Sour cream batter:

- *1 cup sour cream*
- *1 egg*
- *1/3 cup sugar*
- *2 tablespoons all-purpose flour*
- *1/2 teaspoon grated lemon zest*
- *Pinch ground nutmeg*

Crumb topping:

- *1/2 cup all-purpose flour*
- *1/3 cup firmly packed light-brown sugar*
- *1/2 teaspoon ground cinnamon*
- *1/4 cup (1/2 stick) unsalted butter, melted*
- *1/4 cup chopped pecans or walnuts*

Make the pie crust and line a 9-inch pie shell with it, crimping the edge in an attractive manner. Refrigerate for at least 15 minutes.

Fruit compote:

Chop the apricots and peaches. Place in a small saucepan along with the apricot or peach nectar and the liqueur. Bring to a boil over moderate heat; reduce the heat and simmer, stirring often, for 10 minutes. Add the dried cranberries or cherries and continue simmering and stirring until the fruit is tender and the liquid is absorbed. Remove from the heat and let stand while preparing the rest of the pie.

Preheat the oven to 425 degrees.

Sour cream batter:

In a medium bowl, stir together the sour cream, egg, sugar, flour, lemon zest, and nutmeg until well blended. Stir in the dried fruit mixture and spoon the filling into the chilled pie shell.

Crumb topping:

In a small bowl, combine the flour, sugar, and cinnamon. Drizzle in the butter and mix with a fork to moisten. Stir in the nuts.

Scatter the topping in an even layer over the fruit.

Finishing the pie:

Bake the pie for 15 minutes at 425 degrees. Then reduce the oven temperature to 350 degrees. Continue baking 20 to 25 minutes longer, or until the crumbs are golden brown and the filling is almost set. Serve at room temperature.

PUMPKIN PRALINE PIE

A generous one-quarter cup of Liqueur Brûlé in the filling echoes the caramel character of the crunch topping. Serve with lightly whipped cream sweetened with brown sugar and flavored with more of the liqueur.

MAKES ONE 9-INCH PIE, 6 SERVINGS

1 partially baked 9-inch deep pie shell (page 94)

Pumpkin filling:

1 can (16 ounces) canned solid-pack pumpkin (not pumpkin pie filling)

2/3 cup firmly packed light-brown sugar

2 eggs plus 1 egg yolk

1 tablespoon all-purpose flour

1 teaspoon ground cinnamon

1/2 teaspoon ground ginger

1/4 teaspoon ground cloves

1 cup light cream or evaporated milk

1/4 cup Liqueur Brûlé

Praline topping:

1 cup coarsely chopped pecans

1/3 cup firmly packed light brown sugar

3 tablespoons melted butter

Preheat the oven to 425 degrees. Place the pie pan on a cookie sheet. Set aside.

Pumpkin filling:

In a medium bowl, beat together the ingredients in the order given. Pour into the partially baked crust.

Bake the pie for 15 minutes. Reduce the oven temperature to 350 degrees. Continue baking until a knife inserted 1 inch from the center of the pie comes out clean, about 45 minutes longer. Cool the pie completely on a wire rack.

Praline topping:

Preheat the broiler, adjusting the rack 5 inches from the heat.

In a small bowl, mix the pecans and the brown sugar. Drizzle in the butter; then stir to evenly moisten the nut–sugar mixture. Sprinkle the praline topping in an even layer over the completely cooled pie.

Broil, watching very carefully to avoid burning, until the topping bubbles and the nuts turn golden brown, only about 1 to 2 minutes. Serve the pie warm or at room temperature.

DEEP-DISH DOUBLE BERRY PIE

The flavors of blueberries and raspberries meld beautifully under a pastry blanket. Serve with a mixture of softly whipped cream and lemon yogurt.

MAKES ONE DEEP 9-INCH PIE, 6 TO 8 SERVINGS

1/3 cup all-purpose flour

1 cup sugar

3 cups blueberries, rinsed and picked over

1/2 pint fresh raspberries

2 tablespoons Chambord or other raspberry liqueur

1 teaspoon grated lemon zest

2 teaspoons freshly squeezed lemon juice

1 tablespoon unsalted butter, optional

Pastry dough for a deep 9-inch pie (page 94)

Milk, for brushing on the pastry

Sugar, for sprinkling on the pastry

Preheat the oven to 425 degrees. Get out a deep 9-inch pie pan.

In a large bowl, combine the flour and sugar. Add the blueberries and raspberries, liqueur, lemon zest, and lemon juice and toss together gently.

Pile the fruit in the pie pan. Dot with the butter, if desired.

Top the filling with the dough; seal the edges and crimp the rim in a decorative manner. Brush with the milk and sprinkle with the sugar. Cut several steam vents in the dough with a sharp knife.

Bake the pie for 20 minutes; then reduce the oven temperature to 350 degrees. Bake until the crust is golden brown and the juices bubble up, about 30 to 40 minutes longer.

BANANA CREAM PIE

Remember to cloak the just-sliced bananas immediately with the warm custard filling, so they don't discolor.

MAKES ONE 9-INCH PIE, 8 SERVINGS

1 fully baked 9-inch pie shell (page 93)

Pie:

1/2 cup sugar

1/4 cup cornstarch

Pinch salt

1 cup heavy cream

1 cup milk

3 egg yolks, lightly beaten

3   tablespoons unsalted butter, softened

2 firm, ripe bananas

1/4 cup banana liqueur

Whipped cream topping:

1 1/2 cups heavy cream

2 tablespoons powdered sugar

1 tablespoon banana liqueur

Pie:

In a large mixing bowl, whisk together the sugar, cornstarch, and salt. Gradually beat in the heavy cream, then the milk, in a thin, steady stream. Whisk in the egg yolks, one at a time.

Transfer the custard to a medium heavy stainless-steel or enamel saucepan. Cook over moderate heat, whisking constantly and gently, until the mixture comes to a complete boil. Reduce the heat; simmer, stirring occasionally, 2 minutes longer.

Immediately remove the saucepan from the heat and pour the custard into a small bowl. Beat in the butter, a tablespoon at a time, stirring to melt each tablespoon before adding the next. Cover the surface of the custard directly with a piece of plastic wrap. Let cool until lukewarm, about 1 hour.

Peel and slice the bananas on the diagonal into 1-inch pieces. Strew in an even layer over the pastry shell. Stir the liqueur into the lukewarm filling, then immediately pour the filling over the bananas, spreading gently to cover them completely. Refrigerate the pie for 20 minutes.

Whipped cream topping:

In a chilled medium deep bowl with an electric mixer on high speed, beat the cream until it forms soft peaks. Gradually beat in the powdered sugar, then the liqueur, and continue beating until the mixture forms stiff peaks.

Spread the whipped cream in attractive swirls over the custard filling, covering it completely. Refrigerate the finished pie for at least 1 hour.

MACADAMIA CREAM PIE

Hawaii's star product—the macadamia nut—teams up with coffee in this light and creamy dessert.

MAKES ONE 9-INCH PIE, 8 SERVINGS

1 fully baked 9-inch pie shell(page 93)

Pie:

1/2 cup sugar

1/4 cup cornstarch

Pinch salt

1 cup heavy cream

1 cup milk

3 egg yolks, lightly beaten

3 tablespoons unsalted butter, softened

1/4 cup Kahlúa or other coffee liqueur

1/2 chopped macadamia nuts

1 tablespoon instant espresso powder dissolved in 1 tablespoon water

Whipped cream topping:

1 cup heavy cream

1 tablespoon powdered sugar

1 tablespoon Kahlúa or other coffee liqueur

Whole macadamia nuts and ground fresh coffee, for decorating (optional)

In a large mixing bowl, combine the sugar, cornstarch, and salt. Gradually beat in the heavy cream, then the milk, in a thin, steady stream. Whisk in the egg yolks, one at a time.

Transfer the custard to a medium heavy stainless steel or enamel saucepan. Cook over moderate heat, whisking constantly and gently, until the mixture comes to a complete boil. Reduce the heat; simmer, stirring occasionally, 2 minutes longer.

Immediately remove the saucepan from the heat and pour the custard into a small bowl. Beat in the butter, a tablespoon at a time, stirring to melt each tablespoon before adding the next. Cover the surface of the custard directly with a piece of plastic wrap. Let cool until lukewarm, about 1 hour.

Stir the liqueur and chopped nuts into the warm filling, along with the dissolved coffee mixture then immediately pour the filling into the pie shell. Refrigerate for 20 minutes.

Whipped cream topping:

In a chilled medium deep bowl with an electric mixer on high speed, beat the cream until it forms soft peaks. Slowly beat in the powdered sugar, then the liqueur, and continue beating until the mixture forms stiff peaks.

Fit a pastry bag with a large star tip; fill with the cream. Pipe out the cream in a decorative pattern on top of the pie. Decorate with the whole nuts and the coffee powder.

Refrigerate for at least 1 hour.

BAILEY'S IRISH CREAM BROWNIE PIE

Bailey's Irish cream liqueur adds its nuances of coconut and cream to this fudgy pie.

MAKES ONE 9-INCH PIE, 10 SERVINGS

Pastry dough for a single crust (page 94)

1/2 cup (1 stick) unsalted butter

2 squares (1 ounce each) unsweetened chocolate

2 eggs

2 tablespoons Bailey's Irish cream liqueur

1 cup sugar

1 teaspoon vanilla extract

1/3 cup all-purpose flour

1/4 teaspoon salt

1 cup chopped walnuts or pecans

Line a 9-inch pie pan with the pastry, forming a high edge; crimp the edges attractively. Refrigerate the pastry shell while preparing the filling.

Preheat the oven to 350 degrees.

In a small heavy saucepan over moderately low heat, melt the butter and the chocolate. Let cool slightly.

In a small bowl with the electric mixer on high speed, beat the eggs until they are foamy. Gradually beat in the sugar in a thin stream until the eggs are thick and lemon colored. Reduce the mixer speed to slow. Beat in the melted chocolate, then the liqueur and the vanilla. Fold in the flour blended with the salt. Scatter the chopped nuts in the bottom of the pie crust. Pour the filling over the nuts.

Bake the pie until the crust is golden and the filling is no longer jiggly, about 35 minutes. Cool completely on a wire rack. Serve with small scoops of ice cream or with whipped cream flavored with additional Irish cream liqueur.

LEMON ANGEL PIE

A meringue shell holds a rich lemon filling. This dessert should be made at least 12 hours before serving to allow the meringue to soften somewhat.

MAKES ONE 9-INCH PIE, 8 SERVINGS

Meringue shell:

3 egg whites

1/4 teaspoon cream of tartar

Pinch salt

1 cup sugar

Lemon filling:

5 egg yolks

1/2 cup sugar

1 tablespoon grated lemon zest

1/3 cup freshly squeezed lemon juice

2 tablespoons Grand Marnier

1 tablespoon light rum

1 cup heavy cream, for the top of the pie

Lemon slices and chopped skinned pistachios, for garnish

Meringue shell:

Preheat the oven to 275 degrees. Lightly butter a 9-inch pie pan and set aside.

In a small bowl with the electric mixer on high speed, beat the egg whites with the cream of tartar and salt until foamy. Beat in the sugar, 1 tablespoon at a time, and continue beating until the mixture forms stiff peaks.

Spread the meringue in the prepared pie pan, swirling to make an even shell.

Bake the meringue for 1 hour. Turn off the oven but do not remove the meringue shell. Allow it to cool and dry in the oven.

Lemon filling:

In the top of a double boiler or a heat-proof bowl that will fit on top of a saucepan, beat the egg yolks until they are foamy. Slowly beat in the sugar and continue beating until the egg yolks are thick and lemon-colored. Stir in the lemon zest and juice.

Cook the filling over barely simmering water, stirring constantly, until the mixture thickens, about 12 minutes. Remove from the heat and let cool.

Stir the liqueur and the rum into the lemon filling, then spoon the filling into the cooled meringue shell. Cover loosely with plastic wrap. Refrigerate for at least 12 hours.

Serving the pie:

Just before serving time, in a small chilled bowl, beat the cream until it forms stiff peaks. Transfer to a pastry bag fitted with a large star tube and pipe out in a decorative pattern on top of the pie. Or swirl the cream attractively on top of the pie. Decorate with the lemon slices and the pistachios.

DRIED CHERRY AND APPLE TURNOVERS

Like other dried fruits, dried cherries are quintessentially true to their fresh fruit flavor. Serve these turnovers warm, with clouds of softly whipped cream flavored with a little more of the cherry liqueur.

MAKES 20 TURNOVERS

1 pound Golden Delicious apples

1 pound tart green apples, such as Granny Smith or Greening

1/3 cup sugar

1/4 cup (1/2 stick) unsalted butter

1 teaspoon grated lemon zest

Juice of 1 lemon

1/2 cup dried cherries

2 tablespoons cherry liqueur

Butter Crust (page 80)

1 egg, slightly beaten with 1 teaspoon water

Prepare and chill the Butter Crust.

Meanwhile, peel, core, and chop the apples. Place them in a large saucepan along with the sugar, butter, lemon zest, and lemon juice. Cover the saucepan and cook the mixture over medium heat until juices form, about 5 minutes. Uncover the saucepan, add the dried cherries and continue cooking until the apples are almost soft but still hold their shape and most of the liquid has evaporated. Remove the saucepan from the heat and cool the mixture completely. Stir in the cherry liqueur.

Preheat the oven to 450 degrees. Butter 2 or 3 baking sheets.

Roll out the pastry to a 1/8-inch-thick rectangle on a lightly floured surface. Cut out 20 circles with a 4-inch round cookie cutter, or use a pizza wheel to make squares.

Place 1 tablespoon of the filling on each pastry circle or square. Brush the border of the dough with the egg and water mixture. Fold the pastry over, to form semicircles or triangles; press the edges together all around with your fingertips. Repeat the pressing with the tines of the fork.

Brush the tops of the turnovers with the egg mixture. Poke a 1/8-inch hole through the top of each turnover. Place the turnovers, 2 inches apart, on the prepared baking sheets.

Bake in the preheated oven, turning the baking sheets once halfway through the baking time, until the pastry is golden brown, about 20 minutes. Serve the turnovers warm.

PRUNE-APRICOT FOLDOVERS

These are little free-form tarts filled with a cooked dried fruit filling. Serve with a mixture of equal parts crème fraîche and vanilla yogurt flavored with more blackberry brandy and a shake of cinnamon.

MAKES 9 TARTS

Prune-apricot filling:

1 1/2 cups pitted prunes

Boiling water

1 cup dried apricots

1/4 cup sugar

1 stick cinnamon

1/4 cup blackberry brandy

Pastry for a 2-crust pie (page 94)

Milk, for brushing on the pastry

1/4 cup sugar blended with 1/2 teaspoon ground cinnamon, for sprinkling on the pastry

Prune-apricot filling:

Put the prunes in a small saucepan and cover with boiling water. Bring to a boil over moderate heat. Reduce the heat; simmer until the prunes plump up but still retain their shape, about 10 minutes. Drain the prunes, reserving 1/2 cup of the cooking liquid; cool the prunes until you can handle them.

Chop the drained, cooled prunes and the dried apricots. In a small saucepan, combine the fruit with the sugar, cinnamon stick, reserved prune-cooking liquid, and blackberry brandy. Bring to a boil over moderate heat; reduce the heat and simmer until thickened, about 5 minutes longer. Remove from the heat and cool completely. Remove the cinnamon stick.

Preheat the oven to 400 degrees.

Roll out the dough to 1/4-inch thickness on a lightly floured surface. Cut it into 5-inch circles. Fill the center of each circle with 3 tablespoons of the filling.

Brush the edge of each circle with the milk. Fold up and pleat the dough in 6 or 7 places, to partially enclose the filling.

Place the foldovers on 2 cookie sheets. Brush the dough edges with more milk and sprinkle with the cinnamon sugar.

Bake the foldovers until the pastry is golden brown and the filling bubbles up, about 20 minutes. Serve warm or at room temperature.

FULLY BAKED PASTRY SHELL

1 1/2 cups all-purpose flour

3 tablespoons sugar

1/8 teaspoon salt

1/2 cup (1 stick) unsalted butter, chilled and cut into 8 pieces

2 tablespoons solid vegetable shortening, chilled

3 tablespoons ice water

Combine the flour, sugar and salt in the work-bowl of a food processor. Cover and pulse to blend.

Add the butter and shortening to the work-bowl. Cover and pulse-chop until the mixture forms a cornmeal-like consistency, no more than 10 times.

Drizzle the water over the butter-flour mixture. Cover and pulse until the mixture comes together, no longer than 5 or 7 times. Remove the dough from the processor. Transfer to a piece of wax paper; form into a flattened disk. Wrap and chill for at least 1 hour.

Roll out the dough to a 12-inch circle on a lightly floured surface. For a tart shell, fit the dough into a 10-inch tart pan, trimming the edge of the dough even with the rim of the pan. For a pie shell, fit the dough into a 9- or 10-inch pie pan, trim a 1- to 2-inch overhang; fold the overhang up; pinch to seal and flute the edge. Chill the dough-filled pan for 1 hour.

Preheat the oven to 425 degrees.

Prick the chilled pastry all over with a fork. Line the pastry shell with aluminum foil or parchment paper; fill with raw rice and/or beans to serve as weights.

Bake until the pastry is set, about 8 minutes. Carefully remove the foil or paper and rice and/or beans. Continue baking the pastry until it is golden, about 12 to 15 minutes longer. Cool completely.

UNBAKED AND PARTIALLY BAKED PASTRY SHELL

For 1 crust

1 1/4 *cups all-purpose flour*

1/4 *teaspoon salt*

1/4 *cup (1/2 stick) unsalted butter, cut into pieces and frozen*

1/4 *cup frozen solid vegetable shortening (measure before freezing)*

3 *tablespoons ice water*

Combine the flour and salt in the workbowl of a food processor. Cover and pulse to blend.

Add the butter and shortening to the workbowl. Cover and pulse-chop until the mixture forms a cornmeal-like consistency, no more than 10 times.

With motor on, drizzle the water through the feed tube. Cover and pulse until the mixture forms a crumbly dough (do not allow to form into a ball), no longer than 5 or 7 times. Remove the dough from the processor. Transfer to a piece of wax paper; form into a flattened disk. Wrap and chill for at least 1 hour.

For unbaked pie dough, roll out the dough to a 10-inch circle on a lightly floured surface. Fit the dough into a 9- or 10-inch pie pan, trim a 1- to 2-inch overhang; fold the overhang up; pinch to seal and flute the edge. Chill the dough-filled pan for 1 hour before filling and baking pie.

For partially baked pie dough, follow the above directions, but instead of filling the chilled dough, line the pastry shell with aluminum foil or parchment paper; fill with raw rice and/or beans to serve as weights. Bake until the pastry is set, about 8 minutes. Carefully remove the foil or paper and rice and/or beans. Add designated filling and continue baking.

NOTE: *Double all ingredients for unbaked 2-crust pie dough.* Roll out dough, half at a time. Use second half to top pie after adding filling, then fold overhang of bottom crust over top crust; pinch and crimp together.

LIQUEUR-LACED DESSERTS

Sauced-Up Applesauce • Cranberry Baked Apples

Blackberry Crisp

Pears Poached in Red Burgundy Wine and Cassis

Baked Peaches • Pears with Caramel Cream Sauce

Strawberry-Orange Cup with Raspberry Sauce

Spirited Orange and Prune Compote

Winter Fruit Compote • Summer Fruit Compote

Bananas Foster • Cherries Jubilee • Strawberries Romanoff

Hazelnut Crêpes with Coffee Ice Cream

Profiteroles with Mocha Fudge Sauce

Eggnog Crêpes with Orange Sauce

Chocolate Mint Terrine • Chocolate Orange Mousse

Whipped Chocolate Mousse • Raspberry Mousse for a Crowd

Cannoli Mousse • Nectarine Fool • Double-Berry Fool

Coffee Custards • Crème Brûlée à l'Orange

Rich Rice Pudding • Irish Cream Bread Pudding

Individual Grand Marnier Soufflés

SAUCED-UP APPLESAUCE

Stir apple liqueur into applesauce and top it with a drift of nutmeg-dusted vanilla yogurt.

MAKES 4 SERVINGS

2 cups unsweetened applesauce, preferably homemade

1/4 cup apple liqueur

1 cup vanilla yogurt

Freshly grated nutmeg

In a small bowl, stir together the applesauce and the liqueur. Cover and refrigerate until serving time.

Divide the applesauce among 4 dessert dishes. Top each portion with yogurt. Grate the nutmeg over the top.

CRANBERRY BAKED APPLES

For an elegant touch, serve the apples and their syrup with cranberry liqueur-flavored custard sauce (page 180).

MAKES 6 SERVINGS

1 1/2 cups raw cranberries

1/2 cup cranberry juice cocktail

1/2 cup firmly packed light brown sugar

2 tablespoons cranberry liqueur, rum, or applejack

2 tablespoons unsalted butter

1 3-inch piece stick cinnamon

6 large baking apples, such as Rome Beauty or Golden Delicious

2 tablespoons sugar

Whipped cream, for serving (optional)

Preheat the oven to 375 degrees.

Combine the cranberries, cranberry juice cocktail, brown sugar, liqueur, butter, and cinnamon stick in a small saucepan. Bring to a simmer over moderate heat, stirring continuously. Remove from the heat; let stand 10 minutes.

While the cranberry mixture is cooling, core the apples. Place the apples in a baking pan large enough to hold them in one layer. Stuff the apple cores with half of the cranberries; sprinkle with some of the granulated sugar; repeat with the remaining cranberries and granulated sugar. Pour any remaining cranberries and sauce around the apples.

Bake the apples, uncovered, basting frequently, for 45 minutes, or until they are tender when pierced with a small knife but still intact. Cool until warm or at room temperature, basting once or twice with the sauce. Serve with whipped cream, if desired.

BLACKBERRY CRISP

A cozy dessert that takes well to a custard sauce, sour cream, or a scoop of vanilla ice cream.

MAKES 6 SERVINGS

Fruit:

- 1/2 cup granulated sugar
- 1/4 cup all-purpose flour
- 1 quart blackberries, black raspberries, or a combination of blackberries and/or black raspberries with raspberries
- 1 teaspoon grated lemon zest
- 2 tablespoons blackberry brandy

Crisp topping:

- 3/4 cup all-purpose flour
- 1/4 teaspoon salt
- 1/4 teaspoon ground cinnamon
- 3/4 cup rolled oats
- 1/4 cup firmly packed light-brown sugar
- 1/4 cup (1/2 stick) unsalted butter, cold, cut into pieces

Preheat the oven to 350 degrees. Butter an 8-inch square glass baking dish or a baking dish with similar capacity.

Fruit:

In a large bowl, combine the sugar and the flour. Add the blackberries and the lemon zest and toss gently to coat. Place the fruit mixture in the prepared baking pan. Sprinkle with the liqueur. Set aside.

Crisp topping:

Sift together the flour and the salt into a small bowl. Add all of the remaining ingredients and blend with your fingers until crumbly and well mixed.

Sprinkle the crumb mixture in an even layer over the fruit.

Bake the blackberry crisp until the topping is golden brown and the fruit bubbles up, about 35 minutes. Let stand at least 15 minutes. Serve warm.

PEARS POACHED IN
RED BURGUNDY AND CASSIS

An exquisite ending to a winter meal.

MAKES 4 SERVINGS

1 bottle (1 liter) Burgundy
1 cup crème de cassis
1 cup sugar
4 3-inch strips lemon zest
Juice of 1 small lemon
1 cinnamon stick
4 firm ripe pears
Ice water
1 tablespoon lemon juice
Fresh mint sprigs, for serving
Lemon zest strips, for serving
Crème fraîche for serving (optional)

In a large saucepan, combine the wine, cassis, sugar, lemon zest, and lemon juice, and cinnamon stick. Bring to a boil over moderate heat. Lower the heat and let simmer for 15 minutes.

Meanwhile, carefully peel the pears using a swivel-bladed vegetable peeler, but leave the stems on. Carefully core the pears from the bottom. As you peel and core each pear, drop it into a bowl of ice water mixed with the 1 tablespoon of lemon juice. (This prevents the pears from darkening.)

Drain the pears; add them to the wine mixture. Simmer gently, turning often for about 35 minutes, or just until the pears are tender but not mushy. Remove the pears from the wine to a glass bowl.

Keep simmering the wine mixture until it reduces to a thin syrup, about 15 minutes. Pour the syrup over the pears. Cover and refrigerate.

At serving time, garnish the pears with mint sprigs and lemon zest. Serve with crème fraîche, if desired.

BAKED PEACHES

A simple Italian treatment for summer's ripe peaches.

MAKES 6 SERVINGS

6 *firm, ripe peaches*

16 *amaretti cookies, crushed*

1 *tablespoon sugar*

1 *egg yolk*

3 *tablespoons amaretto, divided*

Few drops peach schnapps (optional)

1 *tablespoon unsalted butter*

1/3 *cup heavy cream*

Preheat the oven to 350 degrees. Butter a large baking dish.

Halve the peaches. Remove and discard the pits. Remove some of the pulp so each peach half has a little hollow.

Chop the peach pulp; place in a small bowl. Add the crushed amaretti, sugar, egg yolk, 1 tablespoon of the amaretto, and the peach schnapps, if used. Stuff the peach halves with this mixture.

Place the stuffed peach halves, stuffing side up, in a single layer in the baking pan. Dot with the butter.

Bake the peaches until the they are tender but still hold their shape, about 30 minutes.

Remove the peaches to a serving platter. In a small pitcher, combine the remaining 2 tablespoons amaretto and the cream. Add any liquid from the baking pan. Pour a little over each serving.

PEARS WITH CARAMEL CREAM SAUCE

Tender baked pears are served warm with a light, almost custardy, sauce.

MAKES 4 TO 8 SERVINGS

Ice and water

1/2 lemon

4 firm, ripe pears

1/3 cup firmly packed light-brown sugar

2 tablespoons unsalted butter

1/3 cup heavy cream

3 tablespoons Liqueur Brûlé, Vanilla Cordial (page 27), amaretto, or Kahlúa

1/4 cup toasted slivered almonds

Preheat the oven to 375 degrees. Butter a large baking dish; set aside.

Squeeze the lemon's juice into a bowl filled with ice and water. Halve, peel, and core the pears, dropping them into the lemon water as you do so.

Drain the pears, reserving 1/4 cup of the lemon water. Place the pears, cut side down, in a single layer in the baking dish. Sprinkle with the brown sugar and dot with the butter. Pour the lemon water around the pears. Cover.

Bake the pears until they are tender but not mushy, about 30 minutes, uncovering them and basting them once or twice, then recovering them.

Transfer the pears to a serving dish or individual serving bowls. Sprinkle with the almonds.

If the baking pan is flameproof, place it over moderate heat. Otherwise, transfer the pan liquid to a saucepan. Add the cream and simmer 3 minutes longer, or until the sauce is somewhat thickened. Swirl in the liqueur and pour a little sauce over each serving.

STRAWBERRY-ORANGE CUP
WITH RASPBERRY SAUCE

This refreshing combination is at its most flavorful when it is removed from the refrigerator about 15 minutes before serving time.

MAKES 6 SERVINGS

1 package (10 ounces) frozen raspberries in light syrup, thawed

2 navel oranges

2 tablespoons raspberry liqueur

1 tablespoon powdered sugar

2 pints fresh strawberries

Purée the raspberries and their syrup in a blender or food processor; strain through a fine sieve into a medium bowl, to eliminate the seeds.

Grate 1/4 teaspoon zest from 1 of the oranges; stir into the raspberry purée along with the liqueur and powdered sugar.

Rinse, hull, and halve the strawberries. Add to the raspberry purée and toss very gently to coat. Cover and refrigerate.

Peel, and slice the oranges. Cover with plastic wrap and refrigerate.

At serving time, arrange the orange slices on 6 dessert plates. Top with the strawberries in purée.

SPIRITED ORANGE AND PRUNE COMPOTE

The components of this refreshing winter compote can be prepared in advance, but assemble the dessert just before serving to preserve its vibrant colors.

MAKES 6 SERVINGS

Candied rind and currants:

1 to 2 navel oranges

1/3 cup sugar

1/2 cup freshly squeezed orange juice

1/3 cup currants

1 tablespoon Grand Marnier or Cointreau

Prunes:

1 package (15 ounces) pitted prunes

1 Earl Grey tea bag

2 slices fresh ginger, peeled

2 whole cardamom pods

4 strips lemon zest

Juice of 1/2 lemon

1 stick cinnamon

Water (to cover the prunes about halfway)

1/3 cup sugar

1/3 cup Crème de Cassis or port

Oranges:

3 navel oranges

Grand Marnier or Cointreau

Sugar

Candied rind and currants:

Squeeze enough juice from the oranges to yield 1/2 cup. With a grapefruit spoon, scrape away the bitter white pith from one of the orange shell halves. Halve this shell; then snip each half into long thin strips with kitchen shears.

Drop the strips into lightly salted boiling water and simmer 10 minutes; drain. Return the strips to the saucepan.

Add the sugar, orange juice, and currants; bring to a boiling. Lower the heat and simmer 1 minute, or until the sugar melts. Remove from the heat and stir in the liqueur. Let the mixture cool completely; then cover and refrigerate.

Prunes:

Bring all of the ingredients to boiling in a medium saucepan. After the liquid boils for about 1 minute, remove the tea bag. Continue simmering the prunes about 3 minutes longer; then remove them with a slotted spoon to a dish. Simmer the syrup in the saucepan another 10 minutes or so, to thicken it. Return the prunes to the saucepan. Let cool, then cover and refrigerate.

Oranges:

Cut away the skin and bitter white pith from the oranges. Halve the oranges, then cut each half into 1/3-inch slices. Place in a bowl; sprinkle with liqueur and sugar to taste. Cover and refrigerate.

Assembling the dessert:

Spoon the prunes and part of their liquid into a serving bowl. Surround with the orange slices. Strew the candied peel and currants over the top.

WINTER FRUIT COMPOTE

This filling compote combines dried and fresh fruits in a brandy-laced syrup. It can be made several days ahead and reheated just before serving. Serve it topped with crème fraîche, vanilla yogurt, or sour cream.

MAKES 6 SERVINGS

1 1/2 cups apricot nectar
1 cup dried apricots
1/2 cup dried pears
1/2 cup golden raisins
1/4 cup pitted prunes
3/4 cup apricot brandy
3 thin lemon slices
2 thin slices fresh ginger
2 tart green apples such as Granny Smith or Greening, unpeeled, halved, cored, and sliced
2 pears, unpeeled, halved, cored and thickly sliced

Mix together the apricot nectar, apricots, dried pears, raisins, and prunes in a medium saucepan. Bring to a boil over moderate heat.

Stir in the brandy and lemon and ginger slices. Lower the heat and simmer for 15 minutes.

Add the apple and pear slices. Continue simmering for 5 minutes longer, or until the fresh apples and pears are tender but still hold their shape.

Remove the lemon and ginger slices. Serve the compote warm.

SUMMER FRUIT COMPOTE

When the summer fruit basket overflows, serve this dramatic combination as a first course or dessert.

MAKES 6 SERVINGS

5 *cups assorted cut-up light-colored fruits, such as peeled and sliced peaches or nectarines, cubed honeydew or cantaloupe melon, cubed pineapple, quartered apricots, peeled and sliced green plums*

2 *cups assorted dark-colored fruits, such as pitted bing cherries, peeled and sliced purple plums, blackberries, blueberries, raspberries*

5 *tablespoons sugar*

3 *tablespoons orange, apricot, and/or peach liqueur*

1 1/2 *tablespoons blackberry and/or raspberry liqueur*

Place the light fruits in a medium bowl, the dark fruits in a small bowl.

Toss the light fruits with 3 tablespoons of the sugar and the orange, apricot and/or peach liqueur. Toss the dark fruits with the remaining 2 tablespoons sugar and the blackberry and/or raspberry liqueur. Cover both bowls and refrigerate for about 1 hour.

At serving time, place the light fruits in a bowl. Add the dark fruits in the center.

BANANAS FOSTER

Flambéed desserts are unfailingly captivating. Brennan's Restaurant in New Orleans serves a version of this flambéed banana dessert tableside, and if you have a portable gas cooking element, you can do the same. If not, the dessert will be somewhat less theatrical but delicious nonetheless.

MAKES 4 SERVINGS

1/3 cup firmly packed light-brown sugar

1/4 cup (1/2 stick) unsalted butter

4 firm ripe bananas, peeled, halved lengthwise, then crosswise, to form quarters just before serving

Pinch freshly grated or ground nutmeg

1/3 cup light rum

1/3 cup banana liqueur

1 pint vanilla or butter pecan ice cream

In a large chafing dish or skillet over moderate heat, combine the sugar and the butter, stirring often, just until they melt together and start to bubble.

Add the banana quarters and sauté, turning often, just until they soften but still hold their shape. Add the nutmeg. Remove from the heat.

In a small saucepan, heat the rum and the liqueur. Pour over the bananas; do not stir in. Using a safety match, carefully ignite the dessert (stand back, light at the edge), spooning the flaming sauce over the bananas until the flames subside.

Spoon the bananas and their sauce around individual portions of ice cream in large dessert bowls. Serve at once.

CHERRIES JUBILEE

This is another hot fruit dessert served with ice cream; the temperature contrast adds to the dessert's appeal.

MAKES 6 SERVINGS

1 can (30 ounces) pitted sweet cherries

Freshly squeezed orange juice

2 tablespoons sugar

1 1/2 tablespoons cornstarch

2 teaspoons grated orange zest

1/2 cup orange and/or cherry liqueur

1 quart vanilla or burgundy cherry ice cream

Into a 2-cup measure, drain the cherry liquid, setting aside the cherries; add enough orange juice to the liquid to measure 1 1/2 cups.

In a large chafing dish or skillet, combine the sugar and the cornstarch. Slowly stir in the liquid to make a smooth mixture.

Cook over moderate heat, stirring constantly, until the mixture thickens and bubbles about 1 minute. Add the reserved cherries and the orange zest; heat until warm.

In a small saucepan, heat the liqueur(s). Pour over the cherries but do not stir in. Using a safety match, carefully ignite the dessert (stand back, light at the edge), spooning the flaming sauce over the cherries until the flames subside.

Spoon the cherries and their sauce around individual portions of ice cream in large dessert bowls. Serve at once.

STRAWBERRIES ROMANOFF

A classic dessert that uses softened ice cream in its sauce.

MAKES 6 SERVINGS

1 pint strawberries, rinsed and hulled

1/3 cup orange liqueur and/or Fraise des Bois (wild strawberry) liqueur, divided

2 tablespoons sugar

1 cup heavy cream, well chilled

1/2 pint good-quality vanilla or strawberry ice cream, softened a little

6 whole strawberries, rinsed but left unhulled, for garnish (optional)

Slice the strawberries into a medium bowl. Sprinkle with half of the liqueur(s) and the sugar; toss gently to coat. (This can be done ahead of time; cover and refrigerate for up to a few hours.)

In a small deep bowl that's been chilled, beat the cream until it forms soft peaks.

In another small bowl, beat the softened ice cream briefly. Fold in the whipped cream and the remaining liqueur(s), then the sliced strawberries.

Divide the dessert between 6 stemmed glasses or bowls. Garnish with the whole strawberries, if desired. Serve at once.

HAZELNUT CRÊPES WITH COFFEE ICE CREAM

Toasting the hazelnuts brings out their singular flavor in this splendid dessert. Toasted blanched almonds may be used instead of the hazelnuts.

MAKES 6 SERVINGS

Hazelnut crêpes:

1/2 cup whole hazelnuts

1/2 cup milk

1/3 cup brewed coffee, cooled

1/3 cup Frangelico and/or Kahlúa

1 teaspoon vanilla extract

1/8 teaspoon almond extract

3 eggs

1 cup all-purpose flour

3 tablespoons unsalted butter, melted and cooled

1 tablespoon sugar

Oil for coating the crêpe pan

1 pint coffee ice cream

Caramel Coffee Nut Sauce (page 193) and/or Mocha Fudge Sauce (page 191)

Toasting hazelnuts:

To toast and grind hazelnuts, place in a single layer in a shallow roasting pan. Bake in a preheated 300-degree oven, stirring occasionally, until the skins darken, loosen and crack, and the nuts are golden brown, about 15 minutes. Cool slightly, then transfer to a tea towel. Cover with the towel and rub vigorously, to loosen the skins.

Remove and discard as much of the skin as possible.

Transfer the skinned nuts to a blender or food processor. Cover and process with on-off pulses, until finely chopped. Remove and reserve.

Hazelnut crêpes:

In the workbowl of a food processor, combine the milk, coffee, liqueur(s), vanilla and almond extracts, eggs with a wire whisk until blended. Add the flour all at once and beat until the batter is smooth and all of the flour has been absorbed. Beat in the hazelnuts, butter, and sugar. Cover the bowl and refrigerate for at least 2 hours, preferably overnight.

To cook the crêpes, bring the batter back to room temperature.

Heat a crêpe pan over moderately high heat until a few drops of water dropped into it sputter. Lightly brush the pan with the oil and continue heating until the oil is hot (do not allow it to get so hot that it starts to smoke). Remove the pan from the heat.

Stir the batter if it has separated. Quickly add about 1/4 cup of the batter to the hot pan, tilting and swirling the pan quickly to distribute the batter in a thin layer on the bottom. Return the pan to the heat.

Cook until the bottom of the crêpe is golden brown, about 1 minute. Loosen the crêpe all around with a metal spatula; turn and cook the second side. Transfer the crêpe to a plate. Continue with the remaining batter and oil as needed, stacking the crêpes between sheets of wax paper as you go along. Keep warm. (The crêpes can be prepared ahead of time up to this point. Cover them with plastic wrap and refrigerate. Rewarm by removing the wax paper from between the crêpes, wrapping the crêpes in aluminum foil, placing them on a baking sheet, and baking them in a preheated 350-degree oven for about 15 minutes.)

Finishing the dessert:

Quickly roll the warm crêpes around small scoops of ice cream. Serve with one or both of the sauces.

PROFITEROLES WITH MOCHA FUDGE SAUCE

The great point about profiteroles—airy pastry bubbles filled with ice cream—is that they can be prepared way ahead of serving time, making them treasured desserts for entertaining. These have a surprise hidden within the ice-cream filling: a tiny spoonful of rich coffee liqueur.

MAKES 8 SERVINGS

Cream puff paste:

- 1 cup water
- 1/2 cup (1 stick) unsalted butter
- 1 teaspoon sugar
- 1/8 teaspoon salt
- 1 cup all-purpose flour
- 4 eggs
- 1 quart vanilla, butter pecan or coffee ice cream
- 1/3 cup Kahlúa (approximately)

Mocha Fudge Sauce (page 191)

Cream puff paste:

Preheat the oven to 400 degrees. Get out 1 large or 2 regular cookie sheets. Set aside.

In a large saucepan over moderate heat, bring the water, butter, sugar, and salt to a full boil.

Add the flour all at once. Cook, stirring vigorously with a wooden spoon, until the mixture forms a thick, smooth ball that leaves the side of the pan clean. Remove the pan from the heat.

Beat in the eggs, one at a time, beating well after each addition. At first, the dough may seem to separate, but with continued beating the eggs will be absorbed. The dough should be shiny and smooth.

Baking and finishing the profiteroles:

Drop the dough by rounded teaspoonfuls into 32 mounds on the baking sheets(s), about 1 1/2 inches apart.

Bake until the profiteroles are firm, puffed, and golden brown, about 35 minutes. Cool completely on the sheet(s) on a wire rack.

Slice the top off of each profiterole and re-move any soft, uncooked dough from the center.

Working with about one fourth of the ice cream at a time, fill each puff with some of the ice cream. Make a shallow hollow in the ice cream; then fill with a demitasse-spoonful of the Kahlúa, smooth over the ice cream to enclose the liqueur, and replace the profite-role top.

Place the profiteroles upright in a single layer in an aluminum foil-lined baking pan that will fit in the freezer. Freeze the profiteroles until the ice cream is solid; then cover them with aluminum foil and keep frozen until serv-ing time.

At serving time, reheat the Mocha Fudge Sauce. Serve the profiteroles in stemmed glass-es, topped with some of the sauce.

ORANGE EGGNOG CRÊPES WITH ORANGE SAUCE

Eggnog liqueur is a rich, sunny yellow drink that can be used in the batter for crêpes and French toast. Here, the crêpes are filled with pastry cream, then quickly baked and splashed with orange sauce.

MAKES 6 SERVINGS

Orange pastry cream:

1 1/4 cups milk

2 3-inch strips orange zest

3 egg yolks

1/4 cup eggnog liqueur

3 tablespoons sugar

3 tablespoons all-purpose flour

Large pinch salt

Crêpes:

1/2 cup milk

1/4 cup eggnog liqueur

1/3 cup water

1 cup all-purpose flour

1 tablespoon sugar

3 eggs

2 tablespoons unsalted butter, melted and cooled

1 3-inch strip orange zest

Pinch salt

1/4 cup (1/2 stick) unsalted butter or vegetable oil, for cooking the batter

Orange sauce:

1 cup freshly squeezed orange juice

1 cup sugar

1/3 cup orange liqueur

Melted butter for brushing on the assembled crêpes

Sugar for sprinkling on the assembled crêpes

Orange pastry cream:

In a small heavy saucepan over moderate heat, scald the milk with the orange zest. Remove from the heat.

Meanwhile, in a small bowl, whisk together the egg yolks, liqueur, sugar, flour, and salt until the mixture is very well blended. Whisking constantly, beat in about one fourth of the hot milk mixture, then the rest. Return everything to the saucepan.

Cook the mixture over moderately low heat, stirring constantly, until it thickens but does not boil, about 5 minutes. Immediately remove the pan from the heat, strain the mixture into a small bowl, cover the surface directly with plastic wrap, and refrigerate for at least 1 hour.

Crêpes:

In a food processor or blender, combine the milk, liqueur, flour, sugar, eggs, melted and cooled butter, orange zest, and salt. Cover and process until smooth, about 30 seconds, stopping the motor once or twice to scrape down the sides of the workbowl with a rubber spatula. Transfer the batter to a bowl. Cover and let stand at room temperature for at least 1 hour (or refrigerate for up to 1 day).

Heat a crêpe pan over moderately high heat until a few drops of water dropped into it sputter. Lightly brush the pan with the butter or oil and continue heating until the butter or oil is hot (do not allow it to get so hot that it starts to smoke). Remove the pan from the heat.

Stir the batter if it has separated. Quickly add 2 tablespoons of the batter to the hot pan, tilting and swirling the pan quickly to distribute the batter in a thin layer on the bottom. Return the pan to the heat.

Cook until the bottom of the crêpe is golden brown. Loosen the crêpe all around with a metal spatula; turn and cook the second side until it is lightly golden. Transfer the crêpe to a plate. Continue with the remaining batter and butter or oil as needed, stacking the crêpes between sheets of wax paper as you go along. (The crêpes can be prepared ahead of time up to this point. Cover them with plastic wrap and refrigerate.)

Orange sauce:

In a small saucepan over moderate heat, cook the orange juice and sugar until the sugar dissolves. Reduce the heat; simmer until the mixture forms a light syrup, about 7 minutes. Remove from the heat. (The sauce can be prepared ahead of time up to this point. Transfer to a small covered container and refrigerate. Warm slightly before adding liqueur in final step.)

Finishing the dessert:

At serving time, preheat the oven to 450 degrees.

Spread about 1 tablespoon of the filling over each crêpe; then fold the crêpes into quarters. Butter an ovenproof serving platter; then align the filled crêpes on the platter. Brush the crêpes with melted butter and sprinkle with sugar.

Bake the crêpes until the sugar crystallizes and the crêpes are hot, about 5 minutes.

In a small saucepan, heat the orange liqueur, carefully ignite it with a safety match (stand back, light at the edge), and pour the flaming liqueur into the orange sauce. Pour the sauce over the crêpes and serve at once.

CHOCOLATE MINT TERRINE

This marbleized dessert is ideal for entertaining a large group because it can be prepared in advance and frozen until just before serving time.

MAKES 12 TO 15 SERVINGS

1 pound bittersweet chocolate, cut up (for a lighter chocolate flavor, use 3/4 pound bittersweet chocolate, 1/4 pound milk chocolate)

4 tablespoons (1/2 stick) unsalted butter

3 cups heavy cream, divided

2 egg yolks, lightly beaten

1/2 cup green or white crème de menthe

1/4 cup sugar

8 French petit beurre cookies, broken up

Few drops liquid green food coloring (optional)

Mint Crème Anglaise (page 181)

Fresh mint sprigs (optional)

In a large heatproof bowl, combine the chopped chocolate, butter, and 1 cup of the cream. Place over simmering water. Heat, stirring, until the chocolate and butter melt. Remove from the heat and cool slightly. Beat in the egg yolks and 1/4 cup of the crème de menthe. Let cool.

Meanwhile, grease a 9- by 5- by 3-inch loaf pan with tasteless vegetable oil, line it with foil, and oil the foil. Set aside.

In a chilled medium bowl, beat the remaining 2 cups cream with the sugar and remaining 1/4 cup crème de menthe until soft peaks form.

Reserve 1/2 cup of the chocolate mixture. Fold the cookies, then half of the whipped cream, into the remaining chocolate mixture; pour half of this chocolate–cookie mixture into the prepared loaf pan.

If white crème de menthe was used, tint the remaining whipped cream a delicate green with a few drops of liquid food coloring, if desired. Spoon the whipped cream over the chocolate–cookie mixture in the pan; drizzle with the reserved 1/2 cup chocolate mixture, then top with the remaining chocolate–cookie mixture. Smooth the top. Cover the loaf and freeze at least 8 hours or overnight. (When the terrine is frozen solid, it may be very well wrapped and kept frozen for up to 2 weeks.)

To unmold the terrine, carefully loosen the top of the terrine around the edge of the pan with a sharp knife. Dip the pan in a larger pan of hot water for 30 seconds. Unmold the terrine; remove the foil. Return the terrine to the freezer until serving time.

To serve, slice the terrine into very thin slices. Serve with the Mint Crème Anglaise and garnish with fresh mint sprigs, if desired.

CHOCOLATE ORANGE MOUSSE

Unlike many chocolate mousse recipes, this one involves cooking the egg yolks until they are frothy and doubled in volume. This technique imparts an especially smooth, light texture to the mousse.

MAKES 12 SERVINGS

1/2 *pound bittersweet or semisweet chocolate, chopped*

6 *extra-large eggs, separated*

1/4 *cup freshly squeezed orange juice*

6 *tablespoons sugar, divided*

1/4 *cup Grand Marnier or other orange liqueur*

Pinch salt

2 *cups heavy cream*

1 *teaspoon grated orange zest (optional)*

Whipped cream, orange zest slivers, and shaved chocolate, for serving (optional)

Place the chopped chocolate in the top of a double boiler set over very hot, not boiling, water. Cover, place the double boiler over moderate heat, and melt the chocolate, stirring occasionally.

Meanwhile, combine the egg yolks with the orange juice and 2 tablespoons of the sugar in a medium heavy saucepan. Cook over low heat, beating vigorously with a wire whisk, until the yolks begin to thicken. Slowly pour in the liqueur. Continue cooking and beating the mixture until it is very thick. Remove from the heat.

Pour the egg-yolk mixture into a large mixing bowl; fold in the melted chocolate.

In a medium or large bowl with an electric mixer on high speed, beat the egg whites with the pinch of salt until they are foamy. Gradually beat in the remaining 4 tablespoons of sugar, a little at a time. Continue beating until the egg whites form stiff, not dry peaks.

In a medium bowl with the mixer on high speed, beat the cream with the optional orange zest until it forms stiff peaks.

Fold the whipped cream, then the egg whites, into the chocolate mixture. Spoon the mousse into a decorative serving bowl. Refrigerate for at least 2 hours, or until serving time.

If desired, decorate the outer edge of the mousse with rosettes or dollops of whipped cream, orange zest curls, and shaved chocolate.

WHIPPED CHOCOLATE MOUSSE

This ultra-rich dessert is really a chilled chocolate sabayon, an adaptation of a chocolate mousse recipe from the classic book Nick Malgieri's *Perfect Pastry*. It's easiest to prepare in a heavy-duty standing mixer. Vary the liqueur and accompanying garnish as desired.

MAKES 8 TO 10 SERVINGS

6 ounces bittersweet or semisweet chocolate, chopped

1/8 cup (1/4 stick) unsalted butter, cut up, softened

3 egg yolks

3 tablespoons sugar

1/3 cup raspberry or other liqueur

1 1/2 cups heavy cream

1 tablespoon dark rum

Unsweetened whipped cream or crème fraîche, whole raspberries and fresh mint leaves, for garnishing the mousse

In a small heavy saucepan over very low heat, melt the chocolate (or melt the chocolate in the microwave oven for 2 to 3 minutes at medium power). Remove from the heat. Beat in the butter, bit by bit, until it melts in. The mixture will be quite thick. Set aside.

Set out a heatproof bowl that will just fit into a saucepan filled with water brought to a simmer, without falling into it. With a wire whisk, beat the egg yolks in the bowl; slowly beat in the sugar, then the liqueur.

Place the bowl over the saucepan. Cook over the simmering water, whisking constantly, until the mixture thickens and increases in volume. Remove from the heat and pour the eggs into a small bowl for the electric mixer.

Beat with the electric mixer on high speed until the eggs cool completely and become very thick. Stir about one third of the beaten egg mixture into the cooled chocolate; stir and fold in the remainder.

Beat the cream and the rum in a small deep bowl with the electric mixer on high speed just until the cream forms soft peaks. Stir about one quarter of the cream into the choco-late mixture; then fold in the remainder.

Pour the mousse into individual stemmed glasses, or into a decorative bowl. Refrigerate until set, about 2 hours.

NOTE: The recipe can be doubled.

VARIATION: For a marbled appearance, once the mousse and cream have been folded together, partially fold in an additional 1/3 cup lightly whipped cream, leaving it in attractive streaks throughout.

RASPBERRY MOUSSE FOR A CROWD

Like the Chocolate Orange Mousse, this dessert is ideal for buffets. It can be made in advance, looks very pretty when served in a lavish crystal bowl, and is a cinch to serve. Because a large amount of cream is involved here, a heavy-duty standing mixer will make the recipe a lot easier to manage.

MAKES 20 SERVINGS

3 packages (10 ounces each) frozen raspberries in syrup, thawed

3 tablespoons sugar

1 1/2 envelopes (1 tablespoon) unflavored gelatin

1 quart heavy cream

3 tablespoons Chambord or other raspberry liqueur

Fresh raspberries and mint sprigs, for serving (optional)

Drain the syrup from the raspberries into a small heavy saucepan. Reserve the raspberries from 1 package; place the remainder in a food processor. Cover and purée until smooth.

Place a fine sieve over the saucepan. Force the puréed raspberries through the sieve, to remove the seeds. Stir in the sugar.

Sprinkle the gelatin over the top of the raspberry purée; let stand 5 minutes, to soften the gelatin.

Place the saucepan over moderate heat. Cook, stirring often, until the mixture is hot and the gelatin dissolves completely. Remove from the heat. Refrigerate until the mixture is as thick as unbeaten egg whites.

In a large bowl with an electric mixer on high speed, beat the cream with the liqueur just until the cream forms moderately stiff peaks. Reduce the mixer speed to low; carefully beat in the cooled raspberry purée, just until it is blended. Remove the bowl from the mixer and fold in the reserved raspberries.

Pour the mousse into a decorative serving bowl. Refrigerate for at least 2 hours, or up to 2 days, before serving. At serving time, garnish the mousse with fresh raspberries and mint sprigs, if desired.

NOTE: The mousse can also be spooned into stemmed glasses.

CANNOLI MOUSSE

This is the cannoli without the shell! In this variation of a recipe by cooking teacher and author Anna Teresa Callen, whipped ricotta cheese is blended with candied fruit and chocolate. For the best flavor and texture, use fresh ricotta cheese; the difference will be noticeable. Serve with crisp cookies, if desired.

MAKES 6 SERVINGS

2 tablespoons mixed candied fruit, rinsed and drained

2 tablespoons golden raisins or dried cherries

1/4 cup orange liqueur or cherry brandy

1 1/2 pounds ricotta cheese

2/3 cup sugar

1/2 cup miniature chocolate chips

In a small bowl, combine the candied fruit, raisins or dried cherries, and orange liqueur or cherry brandy. Cover and let stand for at least 1 hour.

Place the ricotta in a food processor. Cover and process until smooth, stopping the motor once or twice to scrape down the sides of the workbowl. With the motor running, add the sugar through the feedtube.

Stop the motor. Add the fruit and liqueur and the chocolate chips. Cover and process with on and off pulses until blended.

Pour the mixture into a large serving bowl or individual stemmed glasses. Cover lightly and refrigerate until serving time.

NECTARINE FOOL

The name of this dessert of puréed fruit marbled with whipped cream is intriguing, especially since the simplicity of its preparation makes it anything but foolish. Actually, a fool is an old English dessert of fruit cooked/or puréed and swirled with whipped cream.

MAKES 4 SERVINGS

Nectarine swirl:

>   4 soft, ripe nectarines or peaches
>
>   1 tablespoon lemon juice
>
>   1 tablespoon sugar, or more to taste
>
>   1 tablespoon peach schnapps

Whipped cream swirl

>   1 cup heavy cream
>
> 1 1/2 tablespoons powdered sugar
>
>   1 tablespoon amaretto
>
>   1 tablespoon toasted sliced or slivered
>   almonds, for garnishing

Nectarine swirl:

Peel and pit the nectarines. Cut them into a food processor. Add the lemon juice, sugar, and peach schnapps. Cover and process until smooth. Taste and add more sugar, if desired.

Transfer the purée to a medium ceramic or glass bowl. Cover and refrigerate until well chilled, at least a few hours.

Whipped cream swirl:

At serving time, in a small deep bowl beat the cream, powdered sugar, and amaretto until soft peaks form.

Assembling the fool:

Partially fold the whipped cream into the nectarine purée so both form attractive streaks.

Carefully divide the marbleized mixture among 4 dessert bowls or stemmed glasses. Sprinkle the almonds over the top. Serve soon.

NOTE: The recipe can be doubled.

DOUBLE-BERRY FOOL

With frozen strawberries and raspberries on hand, this dessert can brighten even jaded winter palates. If you prefer fewer seeds, purée the raspberries separately and press them through a fine sieve before combining them with the strawberry purée.

MAKES 8 SERVINGS

1 package (10 ounces) frozen strawberries in syrup

1 package (10 ounces) frozen raspberries in syrup

1/4 cup strawberry, raspberry, and/or orange liqueur

2 cups heavy cream

Thaw the strawberries and the raspberries.

Place the strawberries and the raspberries with their syrups in a food processor or blender; add the liqueur(s). Cover and purée just until smooth. Place in a medium bowl; cover and refrigerate until just before serving time. (This can be done up to a day ahead; stir the purée before proceeding with the recipe.)

At serving time, in a large chilled bowl with the electric mixer on high speed, beat the cream until it forms soft peaks. Spoon the cream on top of the berry purée. Gently fold together until the two mixtures are marbleized, not completely blended. Serve soon.

NOTE: The recipe can be halved, using either the strawberries or the raspberries.

COFFEE CUSTARDS

Rich oven-baked custards with a hint of Kahlúa.

MAKES 8 SERVINGS

3 cups heavy cream

2 tablespoons instant espresso powder

2 tablespoons Kahlúa

5 extra-large egg yolks

1/2 cup sugar

Whipped cream flavored with Kahlúa, or vanilla yogurt, for serving

Preheat the oven to 325 degrees. Set aside 8 1/2-cup custard cups or ramekins.

In a medium saucepan over moderate heat, heat the heavy cream until it is hot to the touch. Stir in the coffee until it dissolves, then remove the saucepan from the heat and stir in the Kahlúa.

In a medium bowl with the electric mixer on medium speed, beat the egg yolks to liquefy them. Gradually beat in the sugar and continue beating until the mixture is thickened and light. Reduce the mixer speed to low; then gradually beat in the hot cream until blended.

Strain the mixture through a sieve into a 1-quart measuring cup or pitcher. Pour the custard into the custard cups, dividing evenly.

Place the cups in a roasting pan; add enough hot water to the pan to come halfway up the sides of the cups.

Bake until the custards are firm to the touch when gently pressed in the middle, about 25 to 30 minutes. Remove the cups from the water. Let cool to room temperature, then refrigerate for several hours.

At serving time, top each custard with a rosette of whipped cream or a dollop of vanilla yogurt.

CRÈME BRÛLÉE À L'ORANGE

For a variation on this recipe, substitute the stripped zest of 1 lemon for the orange zest, and raspberry liqueur for the Grand Marnier.

MAKES 6 SERVINGS

3 cups heavy cream

Stripped zest of 1 navel orange

1/4 cup granulated sugar

6 egg yolks

1 tablespoon Grand Marnier, Triple Sec, or other orange liqueur

1 teaspoon vanilla extract

1/2 cup packed light-brown sugar

Preheat the oven to 325 degrees.

In the top of a double boiler over hot water, combine the cream and the orange zest; place over moderate heat. Cook until the cream is scalded (it will form a thin skin on the surface). Add the sugar and stir until it is dissolved.

In a large bowl, stir the egg yolks to break them up. Slowly stir the hot cream into the yolks. Stir in the Grand Marnier and vanilla. Strain the mixture into a shallow, ovenproof casserole; the mixture should be about 1 1/2 inches deep. Place the dish in a large, shallow baking pan. Place the pan on the middle oven rack; pour hot water into the pan so it comes halfway up the side of the casserole.

Bake the for 20 to 30 minutes, until a knife inserted in the center comes out clean. Do not overbake. Remove the casserole from the hot water to a wire rack; cool to room temperature. Refrigerate the custard at least 8 hours or overnight.

Prepare the caramelized sugar topping anywhere from 1 to 6 hours ahead of serving, but not longer or it will soften.

First preheat the broiler.

Sift the brown sugar in an even layer over the top of the chilled custard, so it is a scant 1/4 inch thick.

Broil, 8 inches from the heat, 2 or 3 min-utes, until the sugar melts. Remove the casse-role from the broiler. Cool to room tempera-ture; then refrigerate for 1 to 6 hours. Crack the caramel at the table to serve the créme brûlée.

RICH RICE PUDDING

Studded with raisins, this top-of-the-stove pudding is comfort food at its best. It is not as thick as some rice puddings.

MAKES 8 SERVINGS

1 tablespoon unsalted butter

1/3 cup raw rice

1 quart milk

1 pint heavy cream

1/3 cup sugar

1/4 cup raisins

6 egg yolks

2 tablespoons Tuaca or other orange liqueur

1 teaspoon vanilla extract

Cinnamon sugar for the top of the pudding: 2 tablespoons sugar and 1 teaspoon ground cinnamon

In a medium heavy saucepan over moderate heat, melt the butter. Sauté the rice in the but-ter for about 1 1/2 minutes.

Add the milk, the heavy cream, and the sugar. Bring the mixture to a boil; then reduce the heat to low. Simmer, stirring often, about 55 minutes.

Add the raisins. Continue simmering for another 5 minutes.

Beat the egg yolks in a small bowl; slowly beat in 1 cup of the hot rice mixture, then return this mixture to the pan. Cook stirring constantly, until the pudding is creamy but thick, about 5 minutes.

Remove from the heat; stir in the liqueur and vanilla. Transfer the pudding to a serving dish. Sprinkle with the cinnamon sugar and serve warm, or refrigerate and serve chilled.

IRISH CREAM BREAD PUDDING

Irish cream liqueur fits in very nicely with the custard taste of bread pudding. As a variation, serve the pudding with Spirited Lemon Sauce (page 183).

MAKES 8 TO 10 SERVINGS

Pudding:

    1 loaf stale French bread
    2 cups milk
    1 cup heavy cream
    1/2 cup Irish cream liqueur
    2 tablespoons unsalted butter, softened
    3 eggs
1 1/4 cups sugar
    1 tablespoon vanilla extract
    1/2 cup raisins

Caramel Irish cream sauce:

    1/4 cup water
    1 cup sugar
    1/3 cup freshly brewed coffee
    1/3 cup heavy cream
    1 teaspoon lemon juice
    1/4 cup Irish cream liqueur

Pudding:

Crumble the bread, with the crust, into a large bowl. Stir together in a bowl the milk, cream, and liqueur; then pour the mixture over the bread. Let stand for at least 1 hour, until the bread has absorbed most of the liquid.

Preheat the oven to 325 degrees. Coat a 9-by 13-inch baking pan with the softened butter. Set aside.

In a large bowl, beat together the eggs, sugar, and vanilla until well blended. Pour this over the soaked bread, add the raisins, and mix gently.

Spoon the pudding mixture into the buttered pan, smoothing the top even. Bake the pudding until the top is light brown and the custard is set, about 1 hour.

Caramel Irish cream sauce:

Meanwhile, prepare the sauce: Pour the water into a small heavy saucepan. Add the sugar and let stand until the sugar is wet. Place the saucepan over moderately high heat.

Cook the sugar, swirling the pan occasionally, until the mixture turns nut-brown. Remove the saucepan from the heat.

Right away, averting your face to avoid splatters, slowly pour the coffee and the cream into the saucepan. Return the saucepan to the heat and continue cooking, stirring constantly, until the caramel melts. Remove from the heat and cool.

Stir the lemon juice and liqueur into the sauce just before serving.

INDIVIDUAL GRAND MARNIER SOUFFLÉS

The drama of a soufflé (or in this case, multiple soufflés) never fails to impress.

MAKES 4 SERVINGS

Sugar and butter for the soufflé dishes

Soufflés:

1 1/2 cups milk

1/4 cup (1/2 stick) unsalted butter, melted and cooled

3/4 cup cornstarch

2/3 cup sugar, divided

5 eggs, separated

3 tablespoons Grand Marnier

1 tablespoon grated orange zest

Whipped cream topping:

3/4 cup heavy cream

1 1/2 tablespoons powdered sugar

2 tablespoons Grand Marnier

Powdered sugar, for sprinkling on the just-baked soufflés

Soufflés:

Preheat the oven to 400 degrees. Generously butter four 12-ounce soufflé dishes or ramekins; sprinkle with sugar. Set aside.

In a small heavy saucepan, combine the milk and the butter. Onto a sheet of wax paper, sift together the cornstarch and 1/3 cup of the sugar; stir into the milk.

Cook over moderate heat, whisking constantly, until the mixture thickens. Remove from the heat; whisk in the egg yolks, then the Grand Marnier and orange zest. Transfer the mixture to a large bowl.

In a second large bowl with the electric mixer on high speed, beat the egg whites and a pinch of salt until they are foamy. Beat in the remaining 1/3 cup sugar, a tablespoon at a time, until the mixture forms stiff peaks.

Gently stir about one third of the beaten egg whites into the custard mixture, then gently fold in the remainder, just until no streaks of white remain. Divide the soufflé mixture among the prepared dishes.

Bake the soufflés until they are puffed and firm on top, about 12 minutes.

Whipped cream topping:

While the soufflés bake, in a small chilled bowl beat the cream and the powdered sugar until the cream forms soft peaks. Gradually beat in the Grand Marnier and continue beating until the cream forms stiff peaks.

Dust the just-baked soufflés with powdered sugar; place on doily-lined heatproof plates. Serve at once with the whipped cream.

ICES, ICE CREAMS, AND SORBETS

Quick Tortoni • Chocolate Nut Coupes

Frozen Grasshopper Pie • Chocolate Cherry Bombe

Double Strawberry Cups • Frozen Orange Cups

Irish Cream Parfaits • Mincemeat Ice Cream

Peach Schnapps Ice Cream

Toasted Almond-Coconut Ice Cream

Apricot Earl Grey Ice Cream • Coffee Praline Ice Cream

Very Vanilla Ice Cream • Café Brulot Ice Cream

Hazelnut Ice Cream • Lemon-Raspberry Frozen Yogurt

Blueberry Cassis Frozen Yogurt • Cantaloupe Sorbet

Mexican Chocolate Granita • Espresso Granita

Cassis Sorbet

QUICK TORTONI

Laced with amaretto and topped with a mixture of toasted almonds and crushed amaretti, this dessert can be enhanced even further with a rosette of ice cream and a chocolate-dipped almond.

MAKES 8 SERVINGS

1/2 cup slivered almonds
1 quart best-quality vanilla ice cream
2 tablespoons amaretto
8 amaretti cookies, crushed

Toast the almonds in a single layer on a baking sheet in a 300 degree oven until golden brown, about 20 minutes. Let cool, then finely chop.

In a large bowl, soften, but do not melt, the ice cream by beating it with a large spoon. Quickly but thoroughly fold in all but 3 tablespoons of the almonds and the amaretto.

Divide the mixture between 8 individual ramekins or one 4-cup dish. Cover lightly and freeze until firm.

Remove the tortonis from the freezer about 10 minutes before serving time, to soften slightly. Sprinkle the amaretti crumbs and remaining toasted almonds over the top. Serve at once.

CHOCOLATE NUT COUPES

A touch of almond or hazelnut liqueur added to store-bought fudge sauce makes for an elegant ice cream dessert.

MAKES 4 SERVINGS

1 pint chocolate and/or vanilla ice cream

2 to 3 tablespoons amaretto or Frangelico

1/4 cup chopped almonds or hazelnuts, toasted if desired

1 cup bottled fudge sauce, heated

Scoop the ice cream into 4 dessert bowls.

Stir the liqueur and nuts into the fudge sauce; spoon over the ice cream. Serve at once.

FROZEN GRASSHOPPER PIE

Serve wedges of this pale green pie with softly whipped cream and fudge sauce, if desired. For an extra-speedy recipe, use storebought crusts.

MAKES TWO 9-INCH PIES, 6 TO 8 SERVINGS EACH

1 1/2 packages (8 1/2 ounces each) chocolate wafers

3/4 cup (1 1/2 sticks) unsalted butter, melted

1 1/3 cups milk

1 package (10 1/2 ounces) miniature marshmallows

1/4 cup white crème de cacao

1/4 cup green crème de menthe

1 pint heavy cream

Pulverize the wafers and make 2 crusts with the crumbs and melted butter according to directions on page 78.

In a medium saucepan over moderate heat, bring the milk to a simmer; lower the heat.

Add the marshmallows. Continue heating, stirring constantly with a wire whip, until the marshmallows melt. Watch carefully to avoid burning on the bottom of the pan. Remove the saucepan from the heat and stir in the liqueurs. Pour the mixture into a small deep bowl that could fit in the electric mixer.

Refrigerate the marshmallow mixture until it thickens and is no longer warm.

In a large bowl with the electric mixer on high speed, beat the cream just until medium-stiff peaks form. Do not overbeat or the filling will be difficult to fold together.

If the marshmallow mixture is too stiff to fold together with the cream, beat it with the electric mixer until it softens. Stir about 1/2 cup of the whipped cream into the mixture, then fold this lightened mixture into the remaining cream.

Divide the filling between the two pie shells. Freeze until firm, at least 4 hours or overnight. When frozen, carefully but thoroughly cover the pies with aluminum foil. Return to the freezer until 10 minutes before serving time.

CHOCOLATE CHERRY BOMBE

This is an elegant dessert worthy of a special occasion—chocolate ice cream enclosing a cherry-almond whipped cream filling. It should be made at least 10 hours before serving, and keeps well for up to a week.

MAKES 12 SERVINGS

1/3 cup dried cherries

1/3 cup chopped drained maraschino cherries

3 tablespoons Cherry Heering or other cherry brandy

3 pints chocolate ice cream

1/4 cup crushed amaretti cookies

1 tablespoon amaretto

1 1/2 cups heavy cream

1/4 cup powdered sugar

1/4 cup toasted blanched almonds, chopped (see Note)

2/3 cup miniature chocolate chips or finely chopped semisweet chocolate

1 cup heavy cream whipped with 1 tablespoon powdered sugar, for garnish

Chocolate curls, for garnish

In a small bowl, combine the dried cherries and maraschino cherries with the cherry liqueur. Cover and let stand for at least 2 hours, stirring occasionally.

Meanwhile, remove the ice cream from the freezer. Let stand at room temperature until slightly softened, about 15 minutes.

While the ice cream softens, line a 2-quart bowl with aluminum foil, smoothing the foil as much as possible. Place the bowl in the freezer.

Scoop out 1 cup of the ice cream, transfer to a small bowl, and stir in the crushed amaretti cookies and amaretto. Cover and return to the freezer.

Carefully and quickly spread the remaining ice cream in an even layer around the inside of the foil-lined bowl, to form a shell. Return the bowl to the freezer and freeze until the ice cream firms up, about 2 hours.

In a small bowl with the electric mixer on high speed, beat the cream with the powdered sugar until it forms stiff peaks. Gently fold in the cherry–brandy mixture and the almonds.

Remove the ice cream shell from the freezer. Sprinkle half the chocolate chips all over the inside of the shell, gently pressing them into the ice cream with the back of a large spoon.

Spoon the whipped cream mixture over the chocolate chips, leaving a 1 1/4-cup cavity in the center. Return the bowl to the freezer and freeze until the whipped cream mixture is firm, about 2 hours.

Sprinkle the other half of the chocolate chips into the cavity, gently pressing them into the whipped cream with the back of a large spoon. Return the bowl to the freezer.

Soften the reserved chocolate–amaretti ice cream in the refrigerator for 15 minutes.

Remove the ice cream shell from the freezer. Spoon the chocolate–amaretti ice cream into the cavity, smoothing the top. Cover the bowl with plastic wrap, then aluminum foil. Return the bowl to the freezer and freeze until very firm, at least 4 hours.

To unmold, remove the foil and plastic wrap from the top of the bowl. Unmold the bombe onto a chilled serving platter; carefully peel off the foil. Smooth the surface of the bombe with a spatula dipped in hot water and dried. Decorate the bombe with rosettes of sweetened whipped cream and sprinkle the rosettes with chocolate shavings. Return the bombe to the freezer until serving time.

NOTE: To toast almonds, place in a single layer on a baking sheet in a 300-degree oven until golden brown, about 20 minutes. Let cool, then finely chop.

DOUBLE STRAWBERRY CUPS

A variation on the classic Strawberries Romanoff.

MAKES 6 SERVINGS

1 quart fresh strawberries

2 tablespoons sugar, or to taste

3 tablespoons orange liqueur, divided

1 pint strawberry ice cream

Rinse and pat the strawberries dry; reserve 6 whole ones for a garnish. Hull the remaining berries and halve them directly into a large bowl. Sprinkle with the sugar and 1 tablespoon of the liqueur; toss gently to combine. Taste and add more sugar, if necessary. Cover with plastic wrap and refrigerate at least 1 hour.

At serving time, soften the ice cream. Combine the softened ice cream and the remaining 2 tablespoons of liqueur in a medium bowl until soft and well blended.

Divide the sliced strawberries among 6 individual dessert bowls. Spoon the ice cream mixture over the berries. Garnish with the reserved whole berries.

FROZEN ORANGE CUPS

Although these take a bit of time to make, they are easy and elegant. And once you've prepared them, dessert is a frozen asset, ready when you are.

MAKES 8 SERVINGS

8 navel oranges

3 pints orange sorbet and/or vanilla ice cream

1/2 cup Alizé (passion fruit liqueur) or orange liqueur

Mint leaves, for serving (optional)

With a long, sharp knife, cut off a tiny sliver from the bottom of each orange, so they will not wobble on the plate; cut off the top quarter from each orange. With a sharp paring knife and a grapefruit spoon, scoop out the flesh from the tops and bottoms of the oranges; reserve for another use. Rinse out the orange shells; pat dry with paper towels. Freeze the tops and bottoms until they are firm.

Half-fill the frozen shells with the sorbet and/or ice cream. Drizzle 1 tablespoon of the liqueur into each orange; fill with the remaining sorbet and/or ice cream. Replace the tops. Freeze the filled shells until serving time. (If storing for longer than a few hours, place the oranges in a large airtight freezer container, or loosely but completely wrap each one in plastic freezer wrap.)

At serving time, garnish the oranges with the mint sprigs, if desired.

NOTE: Vary this recipe to suit your taste. Try chocolate ice cream and orange liqueur or lemon sorbet and Cherry Heering liqueur, for example.

IRISH CREAM PARFAITS

For a quick, make-ahead dessert with a touch of elegance, a parfait is just perfect! Use freezer-safe parfait glasses to be on the safe side. Even if you make this at the last moment, you'll emerge from the kitchen cool and collected.

MAKES 6 SERVINGS

1 quart vanilla and/or coffee ice cream

1 cup fudge sauce, such as Mocha Fudge Sauce (page 191)

1 cup Irish cream liqueur

1 cup heavy cream (optional)

1 tablespoon sugar (optional)

6 chocolate-covered coffee beans (optional)

Layer the ice cream, fudge sauce, and liqueur in each of 6 parfait glasses. Cover with plastic wrap. Place the glasses in the freezer for up to 4 days.

If desired, in a small bowl, beat the heavy cream with the sugar until stiff peaks form.

Remove the parfaits from the freezer. Top with dollops of whipped cream, or decoratively pipe out the whipped cream through a pastry bag fitted with a medium star tip. Top each parfait with a coffee bean. Return the parfaits to the freezer until about 10 minutes before serving time.

MINCEMEAT ICE CREAM

This dessert uses up that last bit of mincemeat from the holidays. Cranberry relish can be used instead.

MAKES 6 SERVINGS

1 cup prepared mincemeat

2 tablespoons pear, ginger, apple, or orange liqueur

1 quart vanilla ice cream

In a small bowl, stir together the mincemeat and the liqueur. Cover tightly and refrigerate at least 2 hours, or up to 1 week.

Let the ice cream soften a little in a large chilled bowl. Break it up with a fork; then quickly beat to a creamy, not melted, consistency. Stir in the chilled mincemeat.

Transfer the ice cream to an 8-inch baking pan. Freeze for 1 to 2 hours, or until the ice cream has firmed up.

PEACH SCHNAPPS ICE CREAM

Quick to mix, a wonderful summer treat.

MAKES ABOUT 1 QUART

2 ripe peaches, peeled, pitted, and diced (about 1 cup)

2 tablespoons peach schnapps

1 1/2 cups heavy cream

1/2 cup sugar

In a medium bowl, combine the peaches with the schnapps, mashing a bit with a fork. Set aside.

In a small saucepan, stir together 1/2 cup of the cream and the sugar. Cook over low heat, stirring, until the sugar dissolves. Remove from the heat and pour over the peaches in the bowl along with the remaining cream. Refrigerate the mixture until chilled.

Freeze the mixture in an ice cream maker, following the manufacturer's directions.

NOTE: Apricot or raspberry liqueur or amaretto can be substituted for the peach schnapps in this recipe.

TOASTED ALMOND-COCONUT ICE CREAM

I like to serve this tropically inspired ice cream topped with hot chocolate sauce; it's reminiscent of a frozen Almond Joy candy bar.

MAKES ABOUT 1 QUART

1 2/3 cups flaked sweetened coconut, divided

2 cups milk, approximately

2 cups heavy cream

1/2 cup sugar

6 egg yolks

1/4 cup Liqueur Brûlé

2/3 cup whole natural almonds, toasted and chopped (page 134)

Toast 1 cup of the coconut on a baking sheet in a preheated 325 degree oven until it is golden, about 5 minutes, stirring several times to prevent burning.

In a small heavy saucepan, combine the toasted coconut with the milk. Scald the milk; then remove from the heat. Let stand 30 minutes. Press the mixture through a fine sieve into a small bowl, discarding the coconut. Measure the liquid; add more milk, if necessary, to make 1 cup.

In a medium saucepan, combine the milk, cream, and sugar. Bring just to a simmer.

In a small bowl, whisk the egg yolks just to liquefy them. Whisking constantly, beat in one third of the hot cream mixture, then whisk the yolks back into the saucepan.

Cook over low heat, stirring constantly with a spoon, until the mixture thickens and coats the back of the spoon. Immediately remove from the heat and strain the hot custard into a bowl. Cover the surface of the custard directly with plastic wrap. Refrigerate until cold.

Stir the liqueur into the custard; then transfer to an ice cream maker and freeze, following the manufacturer's directions, adding the remaining 2/3 cup coconut and the chopped almonds as directed.

APRICOT EARL GREY ICE CREAM

The bergamot flavoring of the tea gives a floral accent to the brandy-laced ice cream.

MAKES ABOUT 1 QUART

1 cup (6 ounces) dried apricots

2/3 cup water

2 tablespoons sugar

1 cup milk

2 tablespoons Earl Grey tea

2 cups heavy cream

1/3 cup sugar

Pinch salt

4 large egg yolks

1 tablespoon apricot brandy

In a small heavy saucepan, combine the apricots, water, and the 2 tablespoons of sugar. Bring to a boil over moderate heat. Then reduce the heat and simmer, uncovered, until the apricots are tender, 10 to 12 minutes. (Watch carefully so that the water does not boil away completely.)

Transfer the apricots and any liquid that remains to a food processor. Cover and process until puréed, scraping the side of the workbowl once or twice. Set aside.

In a heavy medium-sized saucepan, combine the milk and the tea. Heat slowly until the milk is hot. Remove from the heat; let stand for 5 minutes. Strain the milk through a very fine strainer and then return it to the saucepan.

Add the cream, the 1/3 cup sugar, and the salt. Cook over moderate heat, stirring frequently with a wooden spoon, until the sugar dissolves completely and the mixture is hot, 5 to 6 minutes. Remove from the heat.

In a medium bowl, beat the egg yolks with a wire whisk, just to blend. Gradually whisk in one third of the hot cream mixture in a thin stream, beating the yolks constantly. Whisk the tempered yolks back into the remaining cream mixture in the saucepan.

Cook over moderately low heat, stirring constantly, until the mixture becomes a thin custard that lightly coats the back of a spoon, 5 to 7 minutes. (Do not let the temperature exceed 180 degrees or the custard will curdle.)

Immediately remove the saucepan from the heat and pour the custard through a fine strainer into a medium bowl. Place the bowl in a larger bowl of ice and water. Cool the custard to room temperature, stirring occasionally.

Stir in the apricot purée and the brandy with a wire whisk, mixing well so the purée is evenly blended. Cover and refrigerate for at least 6 hours, or overnight.

Pour the custard into an ice cream maker and freeze according to the manufacturer's directions.

NOTE: For a subtler tea flavor, heat the milk before adding the tea; then infuse for 5 minutes.

COFFEE PRALINE ICE CREAM

Praline, the classic European nut crunch, turns store-bought coffee ice cream into a special dessert.

MAKES 1 QUART

Praline:

1/2 cup natural (unblanched) almonds

1/2 cup sugar

1 quart best-quality coffee ice cream

2 tablespoons amaretto or coffee liqueur, plus additional for serving (optional)

Toasted almond slices, for serving (optional)

Oil a cookie sheet well and set aside.

Praline:

Combine the almonds and sugar in a small heavy saucepan. Place over low heat; cook, stirring often with a metal spoon, until the sugar melts and turns a deep golden color (watch carefully at this point to avoid burning). Immediately remove pan from heat and quickly pour the almond and sugar mixture onto the oiled cookie sheet, spreading the mixture as thin as possible with an oiled metal spatula. Let stand until the praline cools completely and hardens. (For easier clean-up, soak the pan, spoon, and spatula in very hot water.)

Invert the hardened praline onto a piece of heavy-duty aluminum foil; top with a second piece of foil. Crack the praline into pieces with a hammer. Place a few pieces of the praline into a food processor. Cover and process, stopping the machine and scraping the side of the workbowl with a rubber spatula several times, until the mixture is completely pulverized. Empty the praline powder onto a piece of wax paper or foil; continue processing the remaining praline. (At this point, the praline powder can be stored in an airtight container and stored for several days.)

Soften the ice cream and scoop it into a large glass or ceramic bowl; quickly fold in the praline powder and the amaretto. Cover and return the ice cream to the freezer.

At serving time, drizzle additional amaretto over each portion of ice cream and sprinkle with a few toasted almond slices, if desired.

NOTE: The praline powder recipe can be doubled or tripled. Use extra powder in buttercreams, sprinkled over pudding or ice cream, or folded into lightly whipped cream and used as a topping for pound cake slices.

VERY VANILLA ICE CREAM

Like the little black dress, this ice cream looks good everywhere, whether it's on top of a piece of cake, under a cloak of chocolate sauce, or in a luxurious frosted.

MAKES ABOUT 1 QUART

2 cups heavy cream

1 cup milk

1 vanilla bean, split

1/2 cup sugar

3 egg yolks

2 tablespoons Vanilla Cordial (page 27) or Liqueur Brûlé

1 tablespoon vanilla extract

In a heavy medium-sized saucepan, combine the cream, milk, and vanilla bean. Bring almost to a simmer over moderate heat. Remove from the heat and let stand 30 minutes. Strain the mixture through a cheesecloth-lined sieve into a bowl, pressing hard to release as much of the vanilla flavor as possible.

Return the cream mixture to the saucepan. Add the sugar. Return almost to a simmer over moderate heat, stirring often, until the sugar dissolves. Remove from the heat.

In a small bowl, whisk the egg yolks to lique-fy them. Still whisking, slowly beat in about 1/2 cup of the hot cream mixture, then the remaining mixture. Return everything to the saucepan.

Cook over moderately low heat, stirring constantly with a large heavy spoon, until the custard is thick enough to coat the back of the spoon, about 5 minutes. Do not overcook or the custard will curdle.

Strain the custard into a small bowl. Let cool to room temperature. (To facilitate this, place the bowl in a larger bowl of ice and water and stir it once in a while.) Stir in the Vanilla Cordial and the vanilla extract. Cover and refrigerate at least 4 hours, or until very well chilled.

Pour the chilled custard into an ice cream maker. Freeze the mixture according to the manufacturer's directions.

CAFÉ BRÛLOT ICE CREAM

The classic flavorings for Café Brûlot—orange, spices, and liqueurs—are added to a custard base.

MAKES 1 1/2 QUARTS

2/3 cup finely ground French-roast coffee

1 3-inch piece stick cinnamon

Stripped zest from 1 navel orange

3 whole cloves

2 pints light cream or half-and-half

1 cup sugar

8 egg yolks

1/4 teaspoon salt

1/4 cup Kahlúa

1/4 cup Grand Marnier

In a medium heatproof bowl, place the ground coffee, cinnamon, orange zest, and cloves.

In a small saucepan, scald the cream or half-and-half; pour this over the coffee in the bowl. Cover and let stand for 30 minutes.

Pour the coffee-infused mixture through a sieve lined with a double thickness of cheesecloth into a medium saucepan. Stir in half of the sugar. Scald the mixture again. Remove from the heat.

In a large bowl, beat the egg yolks with a wire whisk; then gradually beat in the remaining 1/2 cup sugar and the salt and continue mixing until thick and lemon colored. Whisking the mixture constantly, slowly add 1 cup of the scalded cream; beat this mixture back into the remaining cream in the saucepan.

Cook over moderate heat, stirring constantly, until the mixture thickens and forms a custard that coats the back of a spoon. Remove from the heat and pour the custard through a sieve into a medium bowl. Cover the surface directly with a piece of plastic wrap; cool to room temperature. Stir in the Kahlúa and Grand Marnier. Refrigerate until cold.

Freeze the custard in an ice cream maker, following the manufacturer's directions.

HAZELNUT ICE CREAM

This dessert is triply blessed with the flavor of hazelnuts. The cream is perfumed with ground toasted nuts before it's cooked into a custard; then the custard base is blended with chopped nuts and Frangelico before it's frozen.

MAKES ABOUT 1 QUART

2 cups heavy cream

1 cup milk

1 cup ground toasted hazelnuts (page 108)

1/2 cup sugar

3 egg yolks

1/4 cup Frangelico

1 teaspoon vanilla extract

1/8 teaspoon almond extract

1/2 cup chopped toasted hazelnuts (page 108)

In a heavy medium-sized saucepan, combine the cream, milk, and ground hazelnuts. Bring almost to a simmer over moderate heat. Remove from the heat and let stand 30 minutes. Strain the mixture through a cheesecloth-lined sieve into a bowl, pressing hard to release as much of the hazelnut flavor as possible.

Return the cream mixture to the saucepan and add the sugar. Return almost to a simmer over moderate heat, stirring often, until the sugar dissolves.

In a small bowl, whisk the egg yolks to liquefy them. Still whisking, slowly beat in about 1/2 cup of the hot cream mixture, then the remaining mixture. Return everything to the saucepan.

Cook over moderately low heat, stirring constantly with a large heavy spoon, until the custard is thick enough to coat the back of the spoon, about 5 minutes. Do not overcook or the custard will curdle.

Strain the custard into a small bowl. Let cool to room temperature. (To facilitate this, place the bowl in a larger bowl of ice and water and stir it once in a while.) Stir in the liqueur and the vanilla, and almond extract. Cover and refrigerate at least 4 hours, or until very well chilled.

Pour the chilled custard into an ice cream maker. Add the chopped hazelnuts and freeze the mixture according to the manufacturer's directions.

LEMON-RASPBERRY FROZEN YOGURT

Surprisingly, these two piquant flavors play off each other beautifully. A scattering of fresh raspberries would be an elegant flourish.

MAKES ABOUT 1 1/2 QUARTS, 6 SERVINGS

3 tablespoons sugar

3 containers (8 ounces each) lemon yogurt

1 tablespoon framboise or other raspberry liqueur

1 tablespoon raspberry preserves

In a medium bowl, mix the sugar into the yogurt until it dissolves; then mix in the liqueur and the preserves.

Transfer the mixture to an ice cream machine. Freeze, following the manufacturer's directions.

BLUEBERRY CASSIS FROZEN YOGURT

A richly colored frozen dessert. Splash with additional cassis and strew with blueberries, if desired.

MAKES ABOUT 1 1/2 QUARTS

2 tablespoons sugar

3 containers (8 ounces each) blueberry yogurt

2 tablespoons cassis

In a medium bowl, mix the sugar into the yogurt until it dissolves; then mix in the liqueur.

Transfer the mixture to an ice cream maker. Freeze it, following the manufacturer's directions.

CANTALOUPE SORBET

Serve this subtly hued sorbet garnished with paper-thin wedges of the melon. Or spread Blueberry Cassis Sauce (page 187) onto individual serving dishes, top with a double scoop of the sorbet, and sprinkle with additional berries.

MAKES ABOUT 1 QUART

2 very ripe cantaloupes (about 1 1/2 pounds each), peeled, seeded, and cubed

7/8 cup sugar

1 cup freshly squeezed orange juice

2 tablespoons Alizé (passion fruit liqueur)

In a food processor, process the cantaloupe cubes until they are smooth. Pour the purée into a large bowl.

In a medium saucepan, combine the sugar with the orange juice. Bring to a boil and simmer, stirring often, until the sugar dissolves. Remove from the heat and stir into the purée. Refrigerate until completely chilled.

Stir the liqueur into the purée. then transfer to an ice cream maker and freeze, following the manufacturer's directions.

MEXICAN CHOCOLATE GRANITA

A hint of cinnamon and orange uplifts the chocolate flavor of this refreshing ice.

MAKES 6 SERVINGS

Granita:

1/2 cup sugar

1/2 cup unsweetened cocoa powder

2 cups water

2 tablespoons white or brown crème de cacao

1 teaspoon vanilla extract

1 teaspoon grated orange zest

1/2 teaspoon ground cinnamon

Whipped cream topping:

1/2 cup heavy cream

1 tablespoon white or brown crème de cacao

2 teaspoons sugar

Ground cinnamon, for garnish

Orange zest slivers, for garnish (optional)

Granita:

In a medium saucepan, combine the sugar and cocoa powder, stirring well to eliminate all lumps from the cocoa. Slowly pour in the water, beating constantly with a wire whisk, until smooth.

Bring the chocolate mixture to a boil over moderate heat, stirring often to help dissolve the sugar. Lower the heat and simmer for 5 minutes. Remove from the heat. Stir in the crème de cacao, vanilla, orange zest, and cinnamon.

Pour the mixture into an 8-inch or 9-inch metal baking pan. Place in the freezer; freeze until the mixture is firm but not solidly frozen. Break up into icy chunks with a fork. Return to the freezer. Freeze until frozen, at least 3 hours.

Whipped cream topping:

At serving time, in a small deep bowl, combine the cream, crème de cacao, and sugar. Beat with an electric mixer on high speed or a wire whisk until the cream forms soft peaks. Let the granita stand at room temperature for 5 minutes; then break it up with a fork. Spoon the chunks into stemmed glasses. Top with the whipped cream. Dust with the cinnamon and, if desired, garnish with the orange zest.

ESPRESSO GRANITA

This granita is adapted from a recipe by Anna Teresa Callen in her classic book, *Menus for Pasta*. As its name suggests, this frozen dessert is granular, a refreshing ending to a hearty Italian meal. Or serve it instead of afternoon coffee during the torrid summer months.

MAKES 6 SERVINGS

4 cups strong, hot freshly brewed espresso

1/2 cup sugar, or to taste

2 tablespoons sambuca or anisette

2 3-inch strips lemon zest

1 cup heavy cream, for serving

In a medium bowl that fits in an electric mixer, combine the hot espresso and sugar and stir well until the sugar dissolves; add the liqueur and lemon zest. Taste and add sugar to taste, if desired. Cool to room temperature, then cover and refrigerate until cool, about 1 hour.

Remove and discard the lemon zest strips. Then freeze the espresso mixture until ice crystals form around the edge of the bowl.

Remove the bowl from the freezer. Beat the espresso mixture with an electric mixer on high speed until slushy. Return to the freezer and freeze for 2 hours; whip again with an electric mixer until slushy. Repeat process one more time. Cover and freeze overnight.

At serving time, in a small bowl with the electric mixer on high speed, beat the cream until stiff.

Spoon the granita into stemmed glasses. Top with dollops of whipped cream and serve at once.

CASSIS SORBET

A chic dessert that ends a meal in a light yet elegant way.

MAKES 6 SERVINGS

1 1/2 cups water

3/4 cup sugar

1 2-inch piece stick cinnamon

1 cup crème de cassis

2 teaspoons grated lemon zest

1 teaspoon grated orange zest

1 tablespoon freshly squeezed lemon juice

1 tablespoon freshly squeezed orange juice

In a small saucepan, combine the water, sugar, and cinnamon stick. Bring to a boil over moderate heat; reduce the heat and simmer for 6 minutes. Remove the pan from the heat; let the syrup cool.

Remove and discard the cinnamon stick. Add the crème de cassis, lemon and orange zests, and lemon and orange juices to the syrup.

Pour the cassis mixture into an 8-inch or 9-inch metal baking pan. Freeze until mushy. Transfer the sorbet to a chilled bowl; beat with a wire whisk just until the ice crystals are broken up. Return the sorbet to the baking pan.

Freeze the sorbet until it is firm but not rock-hard frozen. Break it up with a fork; quickly spoon into stemmed glasses and serve immediately.

COOKIES, CANDIES, AND CONFECTIONS

Ischl Tartlets

Thumbprint Cookies

Double Nut Biscotti • Mocha Kisses

Black Forest Rugalach

Hazelnut Double Chunk Cookies

Walnut Crescents

Blackcurrant Tea and Cassis Brownies

Date-Nut Logs • Apricot Cakelets

Fudge Tartlets

Spirited Truffles • Walnut Kisses

Gingered Almond Raisin Clusters

ISCHL TARTLETS

Ground hazelnuts permeate the dough for these cookie sandwiches overflowing with spirited preserves.

MAKES ABOUT 3 1/2 DOZEN COOKIES

Cookie dough:

2 2/3 cups all-purpose flour

1/2 teaspoon baking powder

1/4 teaspoon ground cinnamon

1/4 teaspoon salt

1 cup (2 sticks) unsalted butter, softened

1 package (3 ounces) cream cheese, softened

1 cup sugar

1 egg

2/3 cup ground toasted hazelnuts (page 108)

Instant Raspberry Cordial Jam (page 174)

Powdered sugar, for sprinkling on the cookie sandwiches

Cookie dough:

Onto a sheet of wax paper, sift together the flour, baking powder, cinnamon, and salt. Set aside.

In a large bowl with the electric mixer on high speed, beat together the butter and cream cheese until well blended. Beat in the sugar, then the egg.

Reduce the mixer speed to slow. Beat in the sifted dry ingredients, then the hazelnuts. The dough will be sticky.

Divide the dough in half. Shape each half into a disk on a sheet of wax paper; wrap the dough in the paper and refrigerate for at least 3 hours, to firm up.

Preheat the oven to 350 degrees. Get out several cookie sheets but do not butter them.

Roll out the dough, half at a time (keep the other half in the refrigerator for easiest handling), to 1/8-inch thickness on a lightly floured surface. Cut the dough into 3-inch circles with a cookie cutter. Place the circles, 1-inch apart, on the cookie sheets. Refrigerate the scraps while rolling out and cutting the second half of the dough, then re-roll and cut this dough into rounds.

Using a 1/2-inch cookie cutter or thimble, cut out the center from half of the cookies.

Bake all the cookies until their edges are lightly browned, about 8 minutes. Let the cookies cool on the cookie sheets on wire racks for 1 minute, then remove with a metal spatula to the racks and cool completely.

Assembling the cookies:

Spread the bottom of each of the solid cookies with a thin layer of the jam. Top with a cut-out cookie, bottom-side down, and press together very gently so the cookies adhere. Place the filled cookies on wire racks. Sprinkle the tops with the powdered sugar. Using a demitasse spoon, add a dab more preserves to the opening of each cookie. Let stand until the sandwiches set a bit; then store between sheets of wax paper in a tightly covered tin.

THUMBPRINT COOKIES

A dab of preserves fills these nut-enrobed nuggets.

MAKES ABOUT 2 DOZEN COOKIES

2 1/4 *cups all-purpose flour*
1/4 *teaspoon salt*
1 *cup (2 sticks) unsalted butter, softened*
1/2 *cup sugar*
2 *eggs, separated*
2 *teaspoons vanilla extract*
1 1/2 *cups finely chopped walnuts or pecans*
Instant Raspberry Cordial Jam (page 174)

Preheat the oven to 350 degrees. Butter 2 cookie sheets.

Onto a sheet of wax paper, sift together the flour and the salt. Set aside.

In a large bowl with the electric mixer on high speed, beat the butter and the sugar until they are light; beat in the egg yolks, then the vanilla.

Reduce the mixer speed to slow. Beat in the flour, half at a time, to form a stiff dough.

With a fork, beat the egg whites in a pie plate until they are foamy. Place the nuts in a second pie plate.

Form the dough, 1 1/2 teaspoons at a time, into balls with your hands. Roll the balls in the egg whites, then in the nuts, to coat them all over.

Place the balls, 2 inches apart, on the prepared cookie sheets. With your fingertip or a thimble, form a hollow in the center of each cookie.

Bake the cookies until they are firm and golden, about 15 minutes. Remove them with a metal spatula to wire racks. Cool completely.

Using a demitasse spoon, neatly fill each cookie hollow with the preserves.

DOUBLE NUT BISCOTTI

These evolved from a recipe in *The New New York Times Cookbook.*

MAKES ABOUT 3 DOZEN COOKIES

Butter and flour for the cookie sheets
- *2 cups all-purpose flour, or a bit more if needed*
- *1/2 cup ground almonds*
- *1 cup sugar*
- *2 extra-large eggs*
- *1/4 cup dark rum*
- *1/4 cup amaretto or Nocello*
- *1 teaspoon vanilla extract*
- *1/2 teaspoon ground cinnamon*
- *2 teaspoons baking powder*
- *1 cup walnuts*
- *1 cup whole blanched almonds*

Preheat the oven to 350 degrees. Lightly grease 2 cookie sheets with softened butter; dust with flour, shaking off the excess.

In a large bowl, combine the flour, ground almonds, sugar, eggs, rum, liqueur, vanilla, cinnamon, and baking powder; beat with a heavy wooden spoon until well blended. Stir in the walnuts and whole almonds. The dough should be soft and a bit sticky, but it should hold its shape when picked up. If it is too runny, add more flour.

With your hands, scoop up half of the dough. Shape into a long cylinder, about the length of a roll of paper towel. Place on the cookie sheet so it does not touch the edge of the pan. Repeat with the second half of the dough.

Bake the dough cylinders for 45 minutes to 1 hour, or until golden brown and firm. They will spread during baking. Remove the cookie sheets from the oven to a wire rack; let stand 15 to 20 minutes.

Carefully loosen the cylinders from the cookie sheets, using metal spatulas or pancake turners. Let stand on a cutting board until almost at room temperature.

With a serrated bread knife, cut each of the cylinders into crosswise slices about 1 inch thick. Place the slices, a cut side up, on the cookie sheets. Return the cookie sheets to the oven to let the cookies dry out and turn slight-ly golden, about 10 to 15 minutes. Let them cool completely before storing them.

MOCHA KISSES

These dainty meringue cookies are chewy on the inside, crisp on the outside. They make an elegant accompaniment to ice creams and granitas.

MAKES 30 MERINGUE COOKIES

2 teaspoons instant espresso powder

1 teaspoon boiling water

1 teaspoon white or brown crème de cacao

1 teaspoon vanilla extract

2 egg whites

1/2 cup sugar

2 tablespoons unsweetened cocoa powder

Preheat the oven to 250 degrees. Line a large cookie sheet with a piece of parchment paper. (See Note.)

In a cup, dissolve the espresso powder in the water. Stir in the crème de cacao and vanilla. Cool the mixture to room temperature.

In a small deep bowl with the electric mixer on high speed, whip the egg whites until foamy. Gradually beat in all but 2 table-spoons of the sugar, 1 tablespoon at a time, alternating with a scant 1/4 teaspoon of the espresso mixture at a time. Continue beating until the mixture forms stiff peaks.

In a small bowl, stir together the cocoa with the remaining 2 tablespoons sugar. With a rubber spatula, quickly but gently fold the cocoa mixture into the meringue, being careful to avoid deflating the beaten egg whites.

Drop the meringue by teaspoonfuls onto the paper-lined sheet. Then bake the kisses until they are firm on the outside but still a bit soft on the inside, 25 to 30 minutes.

While the kisses are still hot, very carefully remove them with a spatula to a wire rack. Cool completely. Store in a container with a loose-fitting lid.

NOTE: Parchment paper eliminates sticking and is specially treated to withstand high oven temperatures. Look for it in cookware shops.

BLACK FOREST RUGALACH

Like most dried fruit, dried cherries have an intense flavor and perfume. Here, they're macerated in cherry liqueur, then blended with chocolate pieces and nuts in a cream cheese dough.

MAKES 48 CRESCENTS

Filling:

- *1 cup dried cherries*
- *1/3 cup Cherry Heering or other cherry liqueur*
- *2/3 cup sugar*
- *6 ounces semisweet chocolate, broken up*
- *2 tablespoons unsweetened cocoa powder*
- *1 teaspoon ground cinnamon*
- *1 cup walnuts (unchopped)*

Dough:

- *1 package (8 ounces) cream cheese, softened*
- *1 cup (2 sticks) unsalted butter, softened*
- *2 cups all-purpose flour*

Large pinch salt

For assembling:

- *1 egg*
- *1 teaspoon water*

Filling:

In a small bowl, combine the dried cherries and the liqueur. Cover and let stand at least 4 hours, or overnight, stirring occasionally.

Dough:

Meanwhile, in a large bowl with the electric mixer on high speed, blend the cream cheese and butter until fluffy, light, and well combined. Gradually beat in the flour and the salt. The dough will be very soft. Divide and flatten the dough into 4 disks; wrap each in a sheet of wax paper or plastic wrap. Refrigerate until firm enough to handle, at least 1 hour or overnight.

Filling:

Drain the cherries, reserving the thickened syrup for another use, such as a topping for ice cream or crêpes. Place the sugar, chocolate, cocoa, and cinnamon in a food processor.

Cover and pulse-chop until the chocolate forms pea-sized pieces. Add the walnuts and drained cherries. Pulse-chop until both are coarsely chopped.

Assembling and baking the rugalach:

Preheat the oven to 350 degrees. In a cup, beat together the egg and water.

Roll out the dough, one disk at a time, on a lightly floured surface, to form an 8-inch circle. Brush with the egg glaze. Sprinkle one fourth of the filling over the top, pressing lightly to adhere the filling to the dough. Cut the circle into 12 wedges with a sharp knife. Roll up each wedge from the outside in, to form a crescent. Tuck in any of the filling that falls out as the dough is rolled. Place the crescents, point side down and 1 inch apart, on ungreased cookie sheets. Brush with additional egg glaze.

Bake the rugalach until golden, 30 to 35 minutes. Let the crescents cool on the cookie sheets on wire racks for 2 minutes. Gently loosen them with a metal spatula and transfer them to racks. Cool completely before storing in airtight containers. The cookies freeze well.

HAZELNUT DOUBLE CHUNK COOKIES

Grinding part of the nuts into a paste intensifies the flavor of these sophisticated cookies.

MAKES ABOUT 6 DOZEN

2 3/4 *cups all-purpose flour*

1 *teaspoon baking soda*

1/2 *teaspoon salt*

2 *cups whole hazelnuts, toasted (see Note)*

1 *cup (2 sticks) unsalted butter, softened*

1 *cup firmly packed light-brown sugar*

1/2 *cup granulated sugar*

2 *eggs*

2 *tablespoons Frangelico*

1 *teaspoon vanilla extract*

1 *cup coarsely chopped semisweet chocolate (about 6 ounces)*

1 *cup coarsely chopped white chocolate (about 6 ounces)*

Preheat the oven to 375 degrees. Butter 2 or 3 cookie sheets. Sift the flour, baking soda and salt onto a sheet of wax paper; set aside.

Place 1 cup of the toasted hazelnuts in a food processor; cover and process until the nuts form a paste, stopping the motor once or twice to scrape down the workbowl with a rubber spatula. Coarsely chop the remaining nuts.

In a large bowl with the electric mixer on high speed, beat the butter, hazelnut paste, and both sugars until very light. Beat in the eggs, one at a time, then the liqueur and vanilla, beating well after each addition. Reduce the mixer speed to slow. Beat in the the flour mixture, then the chopped chocolates and remaining hazelnuts.

Drop the batter by rounded tablespoons, 2 inches apart, on the cookies sheets.

Bake until the cookies are golden on the bottom and firm on the top, about 10 minutes. Let the cookies stand on the cookie sheets on wire racks for 1 minute, then gently transfer them to the racks with a metal spatula. Cool completely. Store in a tightly closed container.

NOTE: To toast and skin hazelnuts, place them in a single layer in a roasting pan or cookie sheet with sides. Bake in a 300 degree oven for 15 to 20 minutes, or until the nuts smell toasted, are golden in the center, and their skins crack.

Rub the nuts between clean tea towels, to loosen and remove as much of their skins as possible. (It's okay if some of the skins stay on.)

WALNUT CRESCENTS

Deeply flavored with vanilla extract and walnut liqueur, these shortbread-like crescents are baked until they're golden, then rolled in vanilla-scented sugar.

MAKES ABOUT 5 DOZEN COOKIES

Vanilla sugar:

1/2 whole vanilla bean
1 1/2 cups powdered sugar
1/2 cup granulated sugar

Cookies:

1 cup walnuts (unchopped)
3/4 cup sugar
1 cup (2 sticks) unsalted butter, softened
2 tablespoons Nocello, Frangelico, or amaretto
2 teaspoons vanilla extract
2 2/3 cups all-purpose flour

Vanilla sugar:

In a food processor, combine the half vanilla bean, powdered sugar, and granulated sugar. Cover and process until the vanilla is pulverized and the granulated sugar is fine. Transfer to a covered container and let stand at least 4 hours. (This can be done up to several days ahead; keep the vanilla sugar tightly covered to preserve its perfume.)

Cookies:

Preheat the oven to 350 degrees.

Combine the walnuts and about 3 tablespoons of the sugar in a food processor. Cover and process until the walnuts are ground.

In a large bowl with the electric mixer on high speed, beat the butter until it is light and creamy. Slowly beat in the remaining sugar. Reduce the mixer speed to moderate; beat in the liqueur and vanilla. Beat in the walnuts, then gradually the flour.

Shape the dough, about 1 1/2 teaspoons at a time, into crescent shapes; place the cookies 1 inch apart on ungreased cookie sheets.

Bake the cookies until they are golden brown, about 30 minutes. Let them cool on the cookie sheets on wire racks for about 1 minute, then very gently roll them in the vanilla sugar. Let them cool completely, then reroll in the sugar. Store the crescents between sheets of wax paper in airtight containers.

BLACK CURRANT TEA AND CASSIS BROWNIES

In this recipe, rich brownies are brushed with a mixture of the tea and cassis, then with a thin layer of black currant preserves, before being covered with a black currant-infused chocolate ganache. Cut and serve the brownies at room temperature, but store them, lightly covered, in the refrigerator.

MAKES 32 SMALL BROWNIES

4 teaspoons black currant-flavored tea, divided

3/4 cup boiling water

2 squares (1 ounce each) unsweetened chocolate

1/2 cup (1 stick) unsalted butter

2 extra-large eggs, at room temperature

3/4 cup sugar

3 tablespoons crème de cassis liqueur

1/2 cup all-purpose flour

1/4 teaspoon salt

1/4 cup black currant preserves

1/2 cup heavy cream

4 ounces bittersweet chocolate, finely chopped (about 2/3 cup)

Preheat the oven to 350 degrees. Butter an 8-inch square baking pan.

In a 1-cup glass measuring cup, pour the boiling water over 2 teaspoons of the tea; let steep for 5 minutes, then strain through a very fine strainer.

In a small heavy saucepan over low heat, melt the chocolate with the butter; set aside to cool for 10 minutes.

In a small bowl with an electric mixer at high speed, beat the eggs until they are well beaten, then gradually beat in the sugar and continue beating until the mixture thickens slightly. Reduce the mixer speed to low; beat in the chocolate mixture, 2 tablespoons of the strained tea, and 1 tablespoon of the crème de cassis. Remove the bowl from the mixer. Fold in the flour mixed with the salt, just until blended. Pour the batter into the prepared pan.

Bake the brownies in the preheated oven until the mixture is shiny and firm on top and begins to shrink from the sides of the pan, about 25 to 30 minutes. Cool for 10 minutes on a cake rack, then brush the top with a mixture of the remaining 2 tablespoons of crème de cassis and 1 tablespoon of the strained tea. Cool completely on the rack.

In a small saucepan over moderate heat, melt the preserves, stirring often to prevent burning. Strain the preserves, then brush over the top of the brownies.

In a small heavy saucepan over moderately high heat, bring the cream to a boil; remove from the heat and stir in the remaining 2 teaspoons of the tea; let steep for 5 minutes. Strain the cream through a very fine strainer and return to the saucepan. Return to a boil, then pour over the chopped chocolate in a small bowl; let stand for 1 minutes; beat with a wire whisk until smooth. Spread the ganache in an even layer over the preserves. Refrigerate the brownies until the ganache is partially set, then score the top into 32 bars.

Store the brownies in the refrigerator, lightly colored with plastic wrap. Serve them at room temperature.

NOTE: Other fruit-flavored teas, liqueurs, and preserves, such as raspberry and apricot, may be substituted for the black currant tea, crème de cassis, and preserves in this recipe.

DATE-NUT LOGS

Halfway between a confection and a cookie, these chewy sweets go well with orange-spice tea.

MAKES 6 DOZEN LITTLE LOGS

1 cup all-purpose flour

3/4 teaspoon baking powder

1/2 teaspoon ground ginger

1/4 teaspoon salt

3 eggs

1 cup granulated sugar

1/4 cup orange liqueur

1 teaspoon grated orange zest

1 package (8 ounces) pitted dates, chopped

1 cup pecans, chopped

Powdered sugar, for coating the baked logs

Preheat the oven to 350 degrees. Butter a 9- by 13-inch baking pan. Set aside.

Onto a sheet of wax paper, sift together the flour, baking powder, ginger, and salt. Set aside.

In a large bowl with the electric mixer on high speed, beat the eggs until they are foamy. Gradually beat in the granulated sugar and continue beating until the mixture is very thick and forms a ribbon when the beaters are lifted from it. On low speed, beat in the flour mixture just until absorbed. Beat in the liqueur and the zest.

Remove the bowl from the mixer and fold in the dates and nuts. Spread the mixture in the prepared pan, smoothing the top even.

Bake until the top springs back when lightly pressed with a fingertip, about 25 minutes. Cool in the pan on a wire rack for 20 minutes.

With a sharp knife, cut 9 lengthwise strips and 8 crosswise ones, forming 6 dozen tiny rectangles.

Sift the powdered sugar onto a sheet of wax paper. Gently roll the rectangles in the sugar, coating all sides and forming log shapes. Store the cookies in tightly covered containers.

APRICOT CAKELETS

Little liqueur-bathed cakes, one per serving.

MAKES 6 CAKELETS

Cakelets:

1/2 cup dried apricots

1/2 cup apricot nectar

1/4 cup sugar

  2 tablespoons apricot liqueur

1/2 cup all-purpose flour

1/2 teaspoon baking powder

1/8 teaspoon salt

  6 tablespoons (3/4 stick) unsalted butter, softened

  1 egg

  1 teaspoon vanilla extract

Topping:

  1 cup apricot yogurt

  1 tablespoon honey

  1 tablespoon apricot liqueur

Cakelets:

In a small saucepan, combine the apricots, apricot nectar, and half the sugar. Bring to a boil over moderate heat. Reduce the heat and simmer for 1 minute. Then remove from the heat and stir in the liqueur. Let stand for 5 minutes, then drain the fruit, reserving the cooking liquid. Chop the apricots and set aside.

Preheat the oven to 350 degrees. Butter 6 muffin tins and set aside.

Onto a sheet of wax paper, sift together the flour, baking powder, and salt. Set aside.

In a small bowl with the electric mixer on high speed, beat the butter and the remaining sugar until the mixture is very light. Beat in the egg, then the vanilla.

Reduce the mixer speed to slow. Beat in the sifted flour mixture just until it is absorbed. Divide the batter among the prepared muffin tins, smoothing the tops even.

Bake the cakelets until they spring back when lightly pressed with a fingertip and a skewer inserted in the center of one of them comes out clean, about 15 to 18 minutes.

Meanwhile, simmer the reserved cooking liquid until it is reduced to a thin syrup.

Topping:

In a small bowl, combine the yogurt, honey, and liqueur. Refrigerate until serving time.

Finishing the cakelets:

Gently loosen the cakelets from the tins and put them on a wire rack. Brush them all over with the warm syrup. Let them stand for 5 minutes and serve warm. Or cool them completely and serve at room temperature. Spoon the topping over each cakelet.

The cakelets will keep well for a few days if wrapped in plastic and refrigerated.

FUDGE TARTLETS

Use your choice of liqueurs in this recipe. A teaspoon of grated orange zest is nice if you use the orange liqueur; a small handful of chopped walnuts enhances a Nocello-laced filling. More a confection than a cookie, these dainty morsels look lovely topped with candied violets, shaved white chocolate and/or cocoa powder. Since they are hand-formed, these take a while to prepare.

MAKES 4 DOZEN TARTLETS

Cream cheese dough:

    1 package (8 ounces) cream cheese,
      softened

    1 cup (2 sticks) unsalted butter, softened

 2 2/3 cups all-purpose flour

Fudge filling:

    2 squares (1 ounce each) unsweetened
      chocolate

    3 tablespoons unsalted butter

    1 egg

    4 ounces cream cheese, softened

 1/2 cup firmly packed light-brown sugar

    1 tablespoon crème de cacao, orange
      liqueur, Nocello or other liqueur

 1/2 teaspoon vanilla extract

Deep chocolate glaze:

    2 squares (1 ounce each) unsweetened
      chocolate

 1/2 cup sugar

    2 tablespoons same liqueur used in filling

    3 tablespoons water

    2 tablespoons unsalted butter

Cream cheese dough:

In a small bowl with the electric mixer on high speed, beat the butter and cream cheese until blended. Reduce the mixer speed; beat in the flour just until blended. Divide the dough into 4 pieces and wrap each piece in plastic; refrigerate at least 4 hours, to firm up.

Preheat the oven to 350 degrees.

Pinch off pieces of the dough; press into 48 small tartlet pans with your fingers. Place the pans on cookie sheets. Bake the tartlet shells until they are firm and slightly colored, about 20 minutes. Keep them on the cookie sheets to cool.

Fudge filling:

Meanwhile, in a small heavy saucepan over very low heat, melt the chocolate and the butter; remove from the heat. In a small bowl with the electric mixer on high speed, beat together the egg, cream cheese, and brown sugar until smooth. Beat in the chocolate, then the liqueur and vanilla, just until blended.

Using a demitasse spoon or 1/2 measuring teaspoon, divide the filling among the cooled tartlet shells.

Return the tartlets to the oven. Bake until the filling sets but is still a bit wobbly, about 10 minutes. Remove from the oven. Cool completely on the cookie sheets on a wire rack.

Deep chocolate glaze:

In a small heavy saucepan over very low heat, melt the chocolate. Add the sugar, liqueur, and water. Bring to a simmer, stirring once or twice. Remove from the heat. Beat in the butter until it melts and the glaze is smooth. Let cool until the glaze thickens slightly.

Carefully loosen the tartlets from the pans with the tip of a sharp paring knife. Place the unmolded tartlets on the cookie sheets. Spoon a dollop of the glaze over the filling in each tartlet. (There will be some glaze left over; use it to dip other cookies or serve it as a sauce.)

Let the tartlets cool completely before storing them in a single layer in tightly closed containers. They freeze well.

SPIRITED TRUFFLES

Use your favorite liqueur in these bittersweet confections. Vary the coating with the liqueur: Ground roast almonds pairs beautifully with amaretto; cocoa powder is a good match for any fruit-flavored liqueur. An assortment of truffles always makes a much-appreciated gift.

MAKES ABOUT 3 DOZEN TRUFFLES

12 ounces bittersweet or semisweet chocolate, finely chopped

1 cup heavy cream

3 tablespoons liqueur

3 tablespoons unsweetened butter, softened

Unsweetened cocoa powder or powdered sugar, for shaping

Ground nuts, crushed amaretti cookies, and/or chocolate sprinkles, for coating, if desired

Place the chocolate in a small bowl.

In a medium saucepan over low heat, bring the cream to a boil; remove from the heat. Pour the cream over the chocolate, immersing it. Let stand for 1 minute, then beat smooth with a wire whisk. Beat in the liqueur, then the butter, until the mixture is completely smooth.

Cover the bowl; refrigerate until the mixture is cold and firm enough to shape, about 3 or 4 hours.

Dust your hands with cocoa and/or powdered sugar, to prevent sticking and melting. Remove half the truffle mixture from the refrigerator; keep the remainder chilled. Working quickly, shape scant tablespoons of the truffle mixture into free-form balls; roll in your choice of coating(s). Place the truffles on a cookie sheet; refrigerate while rolling remaining mixture. When truffles are firm, transfer to an airtight container with sheets of wax paper between the layers. Refrigerate for up to 3 weeks, or freeze for up to 3 months.

At serving and/or gift-giving time, re-roll truffles in coating, if desired. Place in tiny paper candy cups. If they are a gift, include a note telling the recipient to keep the truffles refrigerated or frozen.

WALNUT KISSES

These are the casual candymaker's truffle-chocolate wafer crumbs blended with nuts and liqueur.

MAKES ABOUT 4 1/2 DOZEN KISSES

1 pound walnuts, ground (see Note)
2 1/2 cups crushed chocolate wafer crumbs
1/3 cup crème de cacao and/or Nocello
1/4 cup honey
Powdered sugar

In a large bowl, combine the ground walnuts, chocolate wafer crumbs, liqueur(s), and honey until well blended.

Form rounded tablespoonfuls of the mixture into balls with your hands; then roll the balls in powdered sugar on a sheet of wax paper.

Store the confections in a tightly covered container.

NOTE: To grind walnuts, place, half at a time, in a food processor. Pulse chop until ground but not yet a paste. Remove to the large bowl and repeat with the remaining walnuts. Or, grind the nuts in a nut grinder.

GINGERED ALMOND RAISIN CLUSTERS

Serve these chocolate-covered fruit-and-nut confections after dinner, with liqueur-laced coffee. Keep in mind, too, that they would make a lovely gift.

MAKES ABOUT 2 DOZEN CLUSTERS

1 cup golden raisins

1/3 cup Drambuie or ginger liqueur

1 cup whole blanched almonds

2 bars (3 ounces each) semisweet chocolate, broken up

2 tablespoons minced crystallized ginger

In a small bowl, combine the raisins and the liqueur. Cover and let stand overnight. Drain the raisins well in a sieve, reserving the Drambuie for another use. Pat the raisins dry with paper towels and set aside.

Place the almonds in a single layer on a baking sheet. Toast them in a preheated 350 degree oven until they are golden brown, 10 to 15 minutes. Let the nuts cool; then coarsely chop them.

In a small heatproof bowl over, not in, a saucepan of simmering water, melt the chocolate. Remove the pan from the heat. Stir in the raisins, almonds. and crystallized ginger until they are coated.

Drop tablespoonfuls of the mixture onto a baking sheet lined with buttered wax paper.

Refrigerate the clusters until they harden. Carefully pry them from the wax paper. Store between layers of wax paper in an airtight container.

GIFTS FROM THE PANTRY:

SAUCES, CONDIMENTS, AND PRESERVES

Instant Raspberry Cordial Jam

Cranberry, Tangerine and Dried Apricot Conserve

Fig, Lemon and Bénédictine Conserve

Cointreau Apples • Apple-Blueberry Conserve

Peach Melba Conserve • Pineapple-Strawberry Conserve

Basic Crème Anglaise • Mint Crème Anglaise

Foamy Orange Passion Sauce • Spirited Lemon Sauce

Butterscotch Pecan Sauce • Gingered Peach Sauce

Mixed Berry Coulis • Blueberry Cassis Sauce

Bing-Cherry Sauce • Kiwi-Lime Sauce

Chocolate Honey Sauce • Mocha Fudge Sauce

Quick Apricot Almond Sauce

Caramel Coffee Nut Sauce

INSTANT RASPBERRY CORDIAL JAM

This spirited toast topper makes breakfast or brunch extra special. You could also use it to fill cake layers and cookie sandwiches. The generous amount of liqueur makes a saucelike consistency.

MAKES ABOUT 1 1/2 CUPS

1 jar (12 ounces) best-quality raspberry jam

1 to 2 tablespoons Chambord or other raspberry liqueur

Empty the jam into a small bowl. Stir in the liqueur. Return to the jar, cover, and refrigerate at least 1 day to allow the flavors to blend.

CRANBERRY, TANGERINE, AND DRIED APRICOT CONSERVE

Conserves are adaptable mixtures. They are equally at home atop a slice of toast or alongside the holiday bird. This one is brightly colored and tangy.

MAKES ABOUT 6 CUPS

4 tangerines or 3 navel oranges

1 cup sugar

1 package (12 ounces) raw cranberries

1 package (6 ounces) dried California apricots, chopped

2 tablespoons apricot or cranberry liqueur, or a combination of both

Squeeze the juice from 3 of the tangerines or 2 of the oranges; add enough water to measure 1 cup. Combine the juice and sugar in a heavy medium-sized saucepan. Bring to a boil over moderate heat, stirring once or twice. Turn off the heat.

Remove two 3-inch pieces of zest from the remaining tangerine or orange; set aside. Peel and section the tangerine or orange.

Add the cranberries, apricots, tangerine or orange sections, apricot and/or cranberry liqueur, and tangerine or orange zest to the hot syrup. Cook over high heat, stirring occasionally, for 10 to 15 minutes, or until the cranberries burst. Remove from the heat. If desired, remove the zest, sliver, and return them to the conserve. Otherwise, remove and discard the zest.

Pour the hot cranberry mixture into sterilized jars. Cool, cover, and store in the refrigerator until serving or gift-giving time.

FIG, LEMON, AND BÉNÉDICTINE CONSERVE

An aromatic, sophisticated fig conserve reminiscent of the flavors of the Mediterranean.

MAKES ABOUT 1 1/2 PINTS

1 lemon
2 pints very ripe small figs
1 1/2 cups sugar
2 tablespoons Bénédictine

Halve the lemon and remove the seeds. Place the lemon halves in a food processor; cover and process with on-and-off pulses until coarsely chopped.

Trim the tops from the figs; halve the figs into the processor. Cover and process a few times, to coarsely chop the figs.

Combine the chopped lemon–fig mixture and the sugar in a small heavy saucepan. Bring to a boil over moderate heat; lower the heat and simmer, stirring often, until the mixture thickens.

Remove the saucepan from the heat. Cool the conserve, stir in the Bénédictine, then spoon it into a sterilized jar. Cover and refrigerate.

COINTREAU APPLES

Although it's been said that you can't mix apples and oranges, this recipe proves otherwise. Golden Delicious apples hold their shape when cooked, so they are ideal for this combination, which is great on toast, in crêpes, or as a simple compote-like dessert.

MAKES ABOUT 5 CUPS

5 *Golden Delicious apples*

2 *3-inch strips orange zest*

1 *cup orange juice, preferably freshly squeezed*

1/2 *cup sugar*

1/2 *cup Cointreau or 1/4 cup each Cointreau and apple schnapps*

Peel, core, and cut the apples into eighths. Place the apple slices in a large saucepan along with the orange zest, orange juice, and sugar. Bring to a boil over moderate heat. Lower the heat, cover the saucepan, and simmer until the apples are tender but still hold their shape, about 10 minutes. Remove from the heat.

Gently stir in the liqueur(s), being careful not to break up the apple slices too much. Remove the orange zest strips; sliver them with a sharp paring knife and return them to the apple mixture.

Cool the apple mixture to room temperature. Transfer it to a container or small decorative jars; cover and refrigerate until serving or gift-giving time. The mixture keeps in the refrigerator for up to 1 month.

APPLE-BLUEBERRY CONSERVE

Top cheese blintzes with this thick fruit and nut mixture, then embellish with a dollop of plain yogurt, crème fraîche or sour cream.

MAKES 4 HALF-PINT JARS

3 large tart apples, such as Granny Smith or Greening

3 cups fresh blueberries, rinsed and picked over

3 cups sugar

1/4 cup chopped crystallized ginger, optional

1/4 cup golden raisins

1/4 cup apple schnapps or apple juice

3 3-inch strips lemon zest, slivered

1/4 cup lemon juice

6 tablespoons crème de cassis

3/4 cup chopped pecans

Peel, core, and chop the apples; you should have about 3 cups.

In a large nonreactive saucepan, combine the apples with the blueberries, sugar, candied ginger, raisins, apple schnapps or juice, lemon zest, and lemon juice. Bring to a boil over moderately high heat, stirring occasionally, until the sugar dissolves.

Continue to boil the mixture, skimming the surface and stirring often to prevent sticking and burning, 15 minutes. Stir in the crème de cassis; lower the heat and continue boiling and stirring until the mixture thickens, about 5 minutes longer.

Remove from the heat; stir in the chopped nuts. Immediately pour the hot conserve into 4 hot sterilized half-pint canning jars. Tightly close the caps. Cool, then store in the refrigerator.

PEACH MELBA CONSERVE

A rosy conserve redolent of summer. Try it as a winter shortcake filling, layered with liqueur-flavored whipped cream.

MAKES ABOUT 1 1/2 PINTS

2 cups chopped ripe peaches (about 3 large peaches, peeled, pitted and chopped into 1/2-inch cubes)

1/2 cup plus 2 tablespoons sugar

1/2 pint fresh raspberries

1/4 cup Chambord or other raspberry liqueur

In a small, heavy saucepan, combine the peaches and the sugar. Cover with plastic. Let stand, tossing gently once or twice, at least 1 hour.

Cook the peaches and their juices over moderately low heat, stirring frequently but very gently to avoid burning the fruit, until the sugar dissolves and the mixture darkens and turns clear, about 25 to 30 minutes.

Toss in the raspberries. Continue cooking, stirring constantly, until the mixture is thick, about 10 minutes longer.

Sprinkle the liqueur over the top and stir it in. Remove the saucepan from the heat.

Immediately pour the mixture into 2 hot sterilized 1-pint canning jars. Tightly close the caps. Cool, then store in the refrigerator.

PINEAPPLE-STRAWBERRY CONSERVE

Simply flavored and beautifully hued, this tangy combination is wonderful sandwiched between yellow cake layers.

MAKES ABOUT 2 PINTS

4 cups finely chopped peeled fresh pineapple (one 3-pound pineapple)

2/3 cup sugar

1 pint fresh strawberries, rinsed, hulled and sliced

2 tablespoons freshly squeezed lemon juice

1/4 cup strawberry liqueur

In a large nonreactive saucepan, combine all the ingredients except for the liqueur. Bring to a simmer over moderate heat, stirring; skim surface. Continue simmering about 1 hour, stirring often to prevent sticking.

Remove the saucepan from the heat. Stir in the liqueur.

Immediately pour the mixture into 2 hot sterilized 1-pint canning jars. Tightly close the caps. Cool, then store in the refrigerator.

BASIC CRÈME ANGLAISE

Use this master recipe to prepare your favorite liqueur-flavored custard sauce.

MAKES ABOUT 2 CUPS

1 pint milk
1/4 cup sugar
5 egg yolks
1 to 2 tablespoons liqueur, or to taste

In a small heavy saucepan over moderate heat, scald the milk with half of the sugar.

Meanwhile, in a small bowl, beat the egg yolks with the remaining sugar, just to break them up.

Slowly beat about 1/2 of the boiling milk mixture into the yolks, beating constantly with a wire whip. Beat the yolk mixture into the remaining milk in the saucepan, beating constantly.

Cook over low heat, stirring constantly with a large wooden spoon, just until the mixture thickens. *Do not let the mixture boil or it will curdle!* The sauce will continue thickening as it cools.

Strain the custard sauce into a medium bowl; cool slightly, then stir in the liqueur. Cover the surface directly with a piece of plastic wrap. Chill the sauce until serving time.

NOTE: The recipe can be halved.

MINT CRÈME ANGLAISE

This is an ideal accompaniment to any deeply flavored chocolate dessert, such as the Chocolate Mint Terrine on page 114.

MAKES ABOUT 4 1/2 CUPS

1 quart milk

20 sprigs fresh mint (about 80 leaves), chopped

1/2 cup sugar

10 egg yolks

2 tablespoons green or white crème de menthe liqueur

Few drops liquid green food coloring, if desired

In a medium saucepan over moderate heat, scald the milk with the mint leaves and half of the sugar. Remove from the heat and let stand at least 30 minutes. Strain through a very fine sieve into a medium bowl, then return the liquid to the saucepan.

In a small bowl, beat the egg yolks with the remaining 1/4 cup sugar, just to break them up.

Bring the strained milk to a boil; then turn off the heat. Slowly beat in about half of the boiling mixture into the yolks, beating constantly with a wire whip. Beat the yolk mixture into the remaining milk in the saucepan, beating constantly.

Cook over low heat, stirring constantly with a large wooden spoon, just until the mixture thickens and coats the back of the spoon. *Do not let the mixture boil or it will curdle!* The sauce will continue thickening as it cools.

Strain the custard sauce into a medium bowl; cool slightly, then stir in the crème de menthe. Tint a delicate green with a few drops liquid food coloring, if white crème de menthe was used. Cover the surface directly with a piece of plastic wrap. Chill the sauce until serving time, up to 2 days.

NOTE: The recipe can be halved.

FOAMY ORANGE PASSION SAUCE

Halfway between a sabayon and lightly whipped cream, this sauce is delightful ladled over simple sponge or angel food cakes.

MAKES ABOUT 2 CUPS

2 egg yolks

1/4 cup sugar

Grated zest and juice of 1 orange

2 tablespoons La Grande Passion (passion fruit liqueur)

1 cup heavy cream

In the top of a double boiler or a heatproof bowl, beat the egg yolks with a whisk to lique-fy them. Slowly beat in the sugar, a little at a time, beating well after each addition; then beat in the orange zest and juice.

Place over, not in, simmering water. Cook, beating constantly, until the mixture thickens enough to coat the back of a spoon. Immediately remove from the heat and stir in the liqueur.

Let the custard sauce come to room temperature; then refrigerate it until thoroughly chilled.

In a small deep bowl with the electric mixer on high speed, beat the cream until it forms stiff peaks; do not overbeat. Fold the beaten cream into the egg mixture, just until blended. Taste and add more liqueur, if desired.

SPIRITED LEMON SAUCE

Serve this translucent sauce over baked apples, steamed puddings or pound cake topped with a scoop of vanilla ice cream.

MAKES ABOUT 2 CUPS

2/3 cup sugar

1/4 cup cornstarch

1/4 teaspoon salt

1/2 cup freshly squeezed lemon juice

1 1/2 cups boiling water

2 tablespoons unsalted butter, cut into pieces

2 tablespoons Chartreuse or B & B

1 tablespoon grated lemon zest

In a heavy medium-sized saucepan, combine the sugar, cornstarch, and salt. Slowly stir in the lemon juice until well blended, then pour in the boiling water and add the butter pieces.

Bring the sauce to a simmer over moderate heat. Then lower the heat and simmer, stirring constantly, until the mixture thickens, about 2 minutes.

Remove from the heat. Stir in the liqueur and the lemon zest. Serve warm.

BUTTERSCOTCH PECAN SAUCE

For a special dessert, ladle this sauce over cupcakes that have been split and filled with vanilla and/or butter pecan ice cream.

MAKES ABOUT 2 CUPS

1/2 cup (1 stick) unsalted butter

2 cups light-brown sugar

1/2 cup heavy cream

1 teaspoon lemon juice

1/4 cup Liqueur Brûlé

1/2 cup chopped toasted pecans or almonds (see Note)

In a heavy medium-sized saucepan, combine the butter, brown sugar, cream, and lemon juice. Bring to a simmer over moderate heat.

Cook, stirring often, until the sauce thickens, about 30 minutes. Remove from the heat; stir in the liqueur and the nuts. The sauce keeps well in the refrigerator, but the nuts should be added just before serving, to preserve their crispness.

NOTE: To toast nuts, place them in a single layer on a cookie sheet or in a shallow roasting pan. Bake in a preheated 300-degree oven for about 10 minutes, or until fragrant and golden.

GINGERED PEACH SAUCE

Serve this piquant sauce over a plain cheesecake; garnish with additional peach slices and raspberries. Or layer with frozen vanilla yogurt and raspberries in stemmed glasses.

MAKES ABOUT 1 1/2 CUPS

1 cup peach nectar

2 tablespoons sugar

2 thin slices fresh ginger, peeled

4 large ripe peaches

2 tablespoons peach schnapps

In a medium saucepan, combine the peach nectar, sugar, and fresh ginger. Bring to a boil over moderate heat; then lower the heat and simmer 5 minutes.

Meanwhile, peel, pit, and quarter the peaches.

Add the peach quarters to the simmering mixture. Continue simmering 7 to 10 minutes longer, or until the peaches are very tender. Remove from the heat and cool slightly.

Purée the peaches, ginger slices, and their liquid in a food processor or blender. Pour into a small bowl; stir in the peach schnapps. Cover and refrigerate.

MIXED BERRY COULIS

Come berry season, this zesty sauce adds instant elegance to fruit platters, ice cream extravaganzas, and simple cakes.

MAKES ABOUT 1 CUP

2 cups berries, such as blueberries, raspberries, strawberries, alone or in combination

1 tablespoon sugar

1 tablespoon freshly squeezed lemon juice

1 tiny strip lemon zest

2 tablespoons raspberry liqueur

Combine all the ingredients in a food processor or blender. Cover and process until smooth. Strain through a fine sieve, if desired, to remove seeds. Transfer to a small bowl; cover and refrigerate.

BLUEBERRY CASSIS SAUCE

This deeply colored sauce can be served on top of ice cream, waffles, pancakes, or crêpes. It is particularly striking when layered with vanilla ice cream and lemon sorbet in parfait glasses.

MAKES ABOUT 1 CUP

1 cup blueberries

1/2 cup red currant jelly

1/4 cup sugar

1 tablespoon water

1 1/2 teaspoons cornstarch

1 tablespoon freshly squeezed lemon juice

1/4 cup crème de cassis

In a small saucepan, combine the blueberries, jelly and sugar. Bring to a boil over moderate heat. Meanwhile, in a cup, stir together the water and cornstarch until smooth. Add this to the blueberry mixture when it boils along with the lemon juice and cassis. Cook, stirring constantly, until the mixture is clear, thick and bubbly, about 5 minutes. Remove from the heat.

If desired, force the sauce through a fine sieve into a small bowl. Serve the sauce warm or cold.

BING-CHERRY SAUCE

This simple sauce highlights summer's luscious cherries. Serve it with whipped cream as a pleasant alternative to strawberries on shortcake.

MAKES 4 SERVINGS

1 pound ripe bing cherries

1 cup red currant jelly

2 tablespoons cherry brandy and 2 tablespoons crème de cassis or 1/4 cup of either

Rinse, stem, and pit the cherries; place them in a medium bowl.

In a small saucepan over moderate heat, melt the jelly; stir in the brandy and cassis until well blended. Pour the mixture over the cherries, tossing gently to coat. Let stand at room temperature for several hours, tossing gently when you think of it.

KIWI-LIME SAUCE

To make a refreshing first-course or dessert dish, toss this sauce, enlivened with Midori (a Japanese honeydew liqueur), over a mixture of honeydew and cantaloupe melon balls. For extra color, garnish with additional sliced kiwi and fresh strawberry halves.

MAKES ABOUT 3/4 CUP

2 ripe kiwis
1/4 cup Midori melon liqueur
2 tablespoons freshly squeezed lime juice
Sugar to taste, optional

Peel, trim, and quarter the kiwis. In a food processor or blender, combine the kiwi quarters, liqueur and lime juice. Cover and process until smooth. Taste and add a teaspoon or two of sugar, if desired. Transfer to a small bowl; cover and refrigerate.

NOTE: The recipe may be multiplied.

CHOCOLATE HONEY SAUCE

Toblerone chocolate, with bits of honey nougat and almonds, makes a luxurious sauce for ice cream or poached pears.

MAKES ABOUT 1 1/4 CUPS

8 ounces Toblerone chocolate, chopped

1/3 cup heavy cream

1 tablespoon unsalted butter

1 tablespoon honey

2 tablespoons amaretto

In a small heavy saucepan or in the top of a double boiler, combine the chocolate, cream, butter, and honey.

Cook the sauce over low heat or boiling water until the chocolate and butter melt and the mixture is well blended.

Remove from the heat. Stir in the liqueur. Serve warm or at room temperature. Store the sauce in a covered container in the refrigerator. It will keep for at least 1 week. Since the sauce thickens, reheat it slowly before using it.

MOCHA FUDGE SAUCE

Kahlúa liqueur and instant espresso powder add a deep undertone to this rich sauce. Serve over coffee ice cream and sprinkle with chopped peanuts, if desired.

MAKES ABOUT 1 2/3 CUPS

5 ounces bittersweet or semisweet chocolate, chopped

1 ounce unsweetened chocolate, chopped

3/4 cup heavy cream

1/4 cup (1/2 stick) unsalted butter

1 tablespoon instant espresso powder

1/2 cup sugar

3 tablespoons Kahlúa

In a small heavy saucepan, combine both chocolates, the cream, and the butter.

Cook the sauce over moderate heat until the chocolate and butter melt and the cream boils. Add the coffee powder, then the sugar. Continue cooking, stirring often, until the coffee and sugar crystals dissolve.

Remove from the heat. Stir in the liqueur. Serve warm or at room temperature. Store the sauce in a covered container in the refrigerator. It will keep for at least 1 week. Since the sauce thickens, reheat it slowly before using it.

QUICK APRICOT ALMOND SAUCE

Try this on waffles, along with a generous dollop of lemon yogurt. Or use as a simple filling between plain or nut cake layers that have been brushed with additional liqueur.

MAKES ABOUT 3/4 CUP

1 jar (12 ounces) best-quality apricot jam

2 tablespoons slivered or sliced almonds, toasted if desired

2 tablespoons apricot, peach or amaretto-peach liqueur

In a small saucepan over moderate heat, cook the apricot jam until it liquefies and bubbles for 2 minutes, stirring frequently to prevent burning. Remove from the heat.

Force the jam through a fine sieve into a small bowl. Then stir the almonds and liqueur into the sieved mixture. Serve warm.

Store any leftover sauce in a covered container in the refrigerator. Heat to serve, if desired, or use as a chilled sauce/spread.

CARAMEL COFFEE NUT SAUCE

Serve this transparent sauce over Irish Cream Bread Pudding (page 126) or over Hazelnut Crêpes with Coffee Ice Cream (page 108).

MAKES ABOUT 2 CUPS

1/4 cup water

1 cup sugar

1/3 cup freshly brewed coffee

2/3 cup heavy cream

1/2 teaspoon lemon juice

2 tablespoons Kahlúa and/or Liqueur Brûlé

1/2 cup toasted chopped macadamia nuts or cashews (see Note)

Pour the water into a small heavy saucepan. Add the sugar and let stand until the sugar is wet. Place the saucepan over moderately high heat and cook, swirling the pan occasionally, until the mixture turns nut-brown. Remove the saucepan from the heat. Immediately, averting your face to avoid splatters, slowly pour the coffee, then the cream, into the saucepan. Return the saucepan to moderate heat and continue cooking, stirring constantly, until the caramel melts into the coffee. Remove from the heat and cool.

Stir the lemon juice and liqueur(s) into the sauce.

Just before serving, stir in the toasted macadamia nuts or cashews.

NOTE: The sauce keeps well in the refrigerator, but the nuts are at their crispest if they are added just before serving.

See page 184 for information on toasting nuts.

INDEX